Do I Get to Wear That Neat Hat?

A National Park Ranger's Story

John,
It's been wonderful working with you and the entire Blueprint team. Thank you for supporting my creative mind! /Averiel
ASH

Do I Get to Wear That Neat Hat?

A National Park Ranger's Story

By Helen S. Hossley

SHIRES PRESS
4869 Main Street
P.O. Box 2200
Manchester Center, VT 05255
www.northshire.com

Do I Get to Wear That Neat Hat?
A National Park Ranger's Story

ISBN Number: 978-1-60571-264-2
Second Edition

Building Community, One Book at a Time
A family-owned, independent bookstore in Manchester Ctr., VT, since 1976 and Saratoga Springs, NY since 2013. We are committed to excellence in bookselling. The Northshire Bookstore's mission is to serve as a resource for information, ideas, and entertainment while honoring the needs of customers, staff, and community.

Printed in the United States of America

To two women, whose lives were instrumental in shaping mine.

To Ginger, for our grand adventure together, and our lifelong friendship. I love you deeply.

To my mom, Sally, who, while on this planet, marveled at my stories and adventures. She loved and supported me through it all. Thanks for looking over my shoulder and cheering me on to complete this book. I can still hear your gentle encouragement in my ear. I feel your love, and miss you every single day.

And finally,
To the U.S. National Park Service, for the best job I ever had.

Acknowledgements and Appreciation

Every person who has ever taken the time to write a book understands that, although writing is a solitary process, the end product is a result of a support community.

My deep appreciation goes out to my husband, John, and my children, Averiel and Brooke, for their loving support and understanding every time they heard me say, "I can't do ____ tonight, as I need to be writing my book," and for their sympathy every time they heard me lament over the fact that I *should be* writing. I love you.

To my family and friends who have been patiently waiting for me to complete the tale of this adventure.

To my fabulous editor Patricia Baird Greene. Without Patricia's keen eye and intuition for good storytelling, this book would have been a disjointed collection of my stories, some good, some not so good. Her guidance has helped make the stories into a book, teasing out the details and hidden trajectories, that I had long forgotten, and luckily, was able to retrieve. I am forever grateful for her guiding me into the art of storytelling and helping me to be a better writer.

Introduction

Tulane University, New Orleans, 1988

I was 26 and tired of serving food. My life had become routine and dull after two years managing the Tulane student restaurant for the Marriott Corporation and clocking over 70 hours a week. Work, work, no social life, and a taskmaster boss we affectionately called the 'Cuban Hurricane'. I briefly entertained thoughts of being like her—confident, successful, powerful—yet my dissatisfaction grew. Feeding college students had never been a life goal. And hey, how many times can you drag out of bed at six in the morning to put your heart into scrambled eggs and soggy bacon for two hundred?

Living in New Orleans had been a welcome change for a Yankee from the Adirondacks of Northern New York. The rich culture, music, delicious food, and variety of people inspired me and woke up my senses, but I was young and yearning for more. I was torn between a secure job with steady paycheck and following the wanderlust in my heart, and I wondered if success and fun had to be mutually exclusive.

I'd always had a strong desire to be out West. It started when I was eight and took a trip to Colorado with my Great Aunt Mabel. I fell in love with the Rocky Mountains and ever after yearned to go back. In high school I learned to ski and often lay on my bed romanticizing what it would be like to ski glamorous places like Vail or Aspen. Little did I

know that my desire to ski would become a vehicle to transform my life.

At the end of the Tulane school year I took a big breath, gave my notice, packed my few belongings into my little car and headed northeast. Why northeast when my heart said go west? I couldn't have said exactly, just a feeling. I landed in Washington, D.C. and spent a year there waitressing at a fine French restaurant, saving money and playing in the city. At a Saint Patrick's Day party, I met Virginia Farrar. Ginger was fresh out of the Army, and we quickly realized we were at the same place in our lives—young with no real career and longing for something more.

"I've been thinking about quitting my job," I told her. "And I've been dreaming of skiing out west. Just like, pick up and go. Ski one place, then move on to the next."

"Sounds interesting," she said, surprising me. "I could see doing that, too. How's your car?"

"You mean you could actually tie up loose ends and take an extended trip—with a stranger?" I asked. Questions assaulted me. What would it be like to travel with another person? What if we didn't like each other? Or had arguments? Or she didn't uphold her end of the bargain? By going it alone up to that point, the only personality I'd had to deal with was my own. But how many other people would have the courage to leave everything behind with no guarantees?

Ginger shrugged. "Hey, I've always kind of jumped into things both feet first. I just figure it out as I go along. What's so different about this?"

I was used to trusting my gut feelings. At that moment my gut was telling me that between the two of us, we

had enough wanderlust and chutzpah to set out on a long exploration and not think twice.

I took a deep breath. "Okay, let's do it! What if we start at Thanksgiving at my parent's house in the Adirondacks? We'd be in the Rockies by December snowfall!"

"Amen to that," said Ginger.

We hugged each other and laughed at our craziness.

I could feel the idea catching fire. Over the summer we chattered about plans and, the more we talked, the more real the adventure became. Between the two of us, Ginger and I knew people we could stay with throughout the United States. With two, it would be much more affordable. My entire focus in the next months would be saving money. We headed back to our respective lives with renewed enthusiasm. We had a Plan!

That summer Ginger started going out with a man whom she'd known in the Army. I hoped she would stay the course and not change her mind, then tried to imagine how I would find the courage to go it alone. Before we'd say goodbye on the phone, I'd get up my courage.

"Hey Ginge, still on board with The Plan?"

"Yep, you bet."

"Whew! You know I go back and forth between being scared to death and excited beyond belief."

Ginger laughed. "Hey, if we're having fun, then it's the right thing to do!"

In November of 1989 we drove up to my parent's house in Lyon Mountain, New York for an early Thanksgiving

dinner. That afternoon Ginger and I packed and repacked my two-door Toyota hatchback. Our cache of clothes, ski boots, travel food, knitting bag, sleeping bags, pillows, back packs, maps, guide books, and a collection of eclectic music on cassette left just enough room for driver and passenger. Sets of downhill and cross-country skis rested in the rack on top.

The next day we pointed my Tercel westward, and never stopped. We were after fun and adventure, and along the way we both grew into our lives. How did I transition from itinerant ski bunny and queen of the road to National Park Ranger? Was it some grand design, kismet, or pure luck? You decide as you follow my story.

Ginger (on left) and I, Banff, Canada 1989

·1·

The Journey Westward and Beyond

Ginger and I traveled west in our storage bin on wheels, tracing a drunken line from upstate New York through Buffalo, Indianapolis, Chicago, Madison, and St. Paul, Minnesota.

From St. Paul we headed out to North Dakota and watched the landscape change into the deep reds, browns, oranges, and yellows of the winter Prairie Grasslands. We were not used to viewing this rainbow landscape. So, I found an exit, drove down into a small canyon, parked on the shoulder of the deserted road, and scrambled up an embankment. What opened up before us was a land of colored rock that stretched mile on lonely mile, hues changing with the racing clouds and sunlight. The cold bite of winter soon drove us back into the car, where we settled in to proceed ever westward—I in the driver's seat, Ginger with her knitting bag and the blue and gray sweater she was making for her brother, Doug.

"It sure is beautiful country," I said. "I can understand why it was sacred to the Native Americans."

"Yeah, it is an inspiring place," Ginger replied. A few miles down the road she added, "But it's so lonely —the absolute middle of nowhere. Who'd ever want to live out here? I mean we haven't seen a house in thirty miles."

"Maybe that's the point," I said, "that it's so untouched and pristine."

We crossed the line into Montana. Miles of straight, black road stretched out into what seemed endless flat prairie. I began to understand why the state coined itself 'Big Sky Country'. In all directions, the bright blue dome above us dominated the landscape. We patiently clocked hundreds of miles, watching every minute to catch the moment when the Rocky Mountains first came into view on the horizon.

Ginger pointed and yelled. "There they are! There they are!"

I squinted into the distance and spotted tiny hazy foothills. We broke into wild cheers. The farther west we traveled, the bigger the white and gray mountains grew against shy blue sky.

As we drove, Ginger often studied the map in her role as navigator. "I can't stand it," she finally said as the mountains drew nearer, "Let's ski! I don't care where. If we leave the interstate at Billings and take this southwest route into a town called Red Lodge, looks like there's skiing there."

I agreed and southwest we headed. Usually, if we weren't staying with friends or family, our accommodation of choice was a youth hostel. Red Lodge didn't have one, but we did manage to find a reasonably priced hotel. The next morning, we ate a quick breakfast of Cheerios in our room, then rushed down to the office to inquire where we could ski.

"The Mountain," the man at the desk replied as if we should know.

We looked at each other. Yep, for sure we downhill ski on a mountain. "Well, which mountain and where?" we asked, feeling like we were in a poorly orchestrated comedy skit.

"The Mountain," he said again, and gave us directions as if it were the only one around. We finally got it—that the name of the best place to ski there was simply called, The Mountain.

Our first day of skiing the Rockies could not have been better—bright sun, great snow, long runs, and friendly people. Ginger, whose voice is like an angel, sang every song she knew on the chairlift. I chimed in as supporting chorus. One skier in the chair in front of us turned around to ask if we took requests.

"Sure!" we piped in unison. "We have a great repertoire."

"Okay. How about 'Quinn the Eskimo'?" he said.

We looked at each other. "Uh, how about a different request!"

We all laughed, delighted with ourselves for being so playful. We found a song we could sing the entire length of the uphill ride and jumped off the lift bellowing out the last bit of chorus. And so went the day of skiing, singing and sun – up and down The Mountain, unhindered by the usual long lift lines. We gained more confidence in our abilities with each run, and stopped only when our legs turned to butter, at which point we found that the local bar had two beers waiting with our names on them.

The next day, before we left town, we explored Red Lodge. "Hey, how about we settle here for the winter and rent that adorable little cabin," said Ginger pointing to an old log cabin with a 'For Sale' sign in the yard. It had broken windows, and from the road you could see into it through the spaces between the timbers.

I laughed. "Think I'd rather live in my trusty car," I said as we drove out of town, turning west toward Yellowstone, our next destination, where, Arden, an old Army buddy of Ginger's lived.

The shortest distance between two points is usually a straight line, unless you live in an area that closes seasonal roads as the snow begins to fly. Red Lodge is located on the eastern side of the Rockies. In order to get from there to West Yellowstone, we had to drive in an inverted U back toward Billings, then left onto Interstate 90 until we reached Bozeman, then another left.

Arden Bailey was now a geologist and National Park Ranger during the summer. In the winter, he ran Yellowstone Expeditions, an overnight cross-country skiing experience in Yellowstone National Park. His small trailer on the outskirts of town looked the epitome of a country bachelor pad. Long woodpiles stood as testament to the mountain winter, and on the ground lay more logs in need of splitting. Sitting out front was a 15-passenger van with rust percolating through its faded blue paint in strategic places. It had been converted into a snow track machine. A bearded man with hair in need of a trim, pulled his head from under the hood of this prize possession as we drove up. His clothes, like his hands, were covered in grease. He flashed a warm grin.

After a happy reunion and intros, we followed Arden past several pairs of cross-country skis and snowshoes poised in a snow bank ready for an impulsive trek into the forest. The warmth of a wood fire enveloped us upon entering the trailer. The small living space was filled with camping equipment and provisions for a modest army. Sitting space

was at a premium, but we managed to squeeze between boxes of supplies to sip the beer he offered. Ginger began filling him in on our far-ranging travel plans.

He mentioned that he was getting ready to lead a guided trip for twelve into the backcountry of Yellowstone just after Christmas.

Ginger and I exchanged looks. "Hey, could you use some free labor in exchange for us coming along?" she asked.

He didn't hesitate. "Sure. I'd be thrilled to have you help me with prep. There's only sleeping accommodation for ten, and I need to expand camp for this group."

"Oh no, you know what?" Ginger shook her head and said looking guilty. "I forgot. It would actually be only Helen. I—um—have plans to meet a friend in Seattle over the holidays."

I stared at her, betrayed. Did she expect me to impose myself on a complete stranger? I held my breath as Arden's eyes lingered on Ginger with a flash of disappointment. What had their relationship in the Army been anyway, I wondered.

He raised his eyebrows. "Oh, well now, what kind of friend?"

"You know him—Keith. Remember. From the Army. He'll be visiting his parents in Seattle, and I just thought it would be great to meet him there since we're this far west."

"Oh yeah, I do remember him. Sure I can't persuade you to stay? Guarantee it'll be amazing."

"Nope. I have my tickets already. Helcat will be great. She has restaurant experience, and she's a natural conversationalist." With that, my involvement in the

Yellowstone Expedition trip was sealed. I still felt uncomfortable.

That night we cleared a space on the living room floor for our sleeping bags, and settled in. With Arden out of earshot, I said, "Do you really think it's okay for me to go into the middle of Yellowstone for a week with someone I hardly know?"

"Oh, come on. He's a great guy," Ginger said.

"Look. You tell me. Should I be on guard here? Is he trustworthy? Is he expecting anything in return?"

Ginger let out a boisterous snort. "Helcat, you are so utterly funny. Arden is the most kindhearted and wonderful person I know. Do you think I'd leave you with someone who wasn't?"

"Well, maybe I'm a little bit jealous I'm not going to Seattle with you. Of course, I'd be an unwelcome third wheel."

"How could I invite you along? I'm just a guest in Keith's parents' house."

"I know. I know. I'm just a little bummed to be missing Seattle. And I just wanted to whine a little."

"In that case, would you like cheese and crackers with your whine?"

We both laughed.

"Nope. I'll just sit on my bruised ego," I said.

"For the record, spending a week in Yellowstone with a pro sounds every bit as phenomenal as Seattle."

"It does, doesn't it? Thanks, Ginge."

"Anytime, darling."

The immediate task next morning was to get Arden's snow-van running reliably, but since Ginger and I possessed zero mechanical ability, we left that up to him. He encouraged us to go cross-country skiing and explained that the U.S. Olympic Nordic Ski Team had their winter training at a site nearby, so we decided to break in our skis on the Olympic trails. They were wide, well-groomed and set in a pattern that meandered through the woods. We were not yet acclimated to the six-thousand-foot elevation; we struggled to get up even small hills without stopping to catch our breath. The ski team passed us several times as if we were standing still.

Back at Arden's that afternoon, we found his van assembled, and ready for a test run. After grabbing a quick lunch, we helped pack the Sno-Coach with supplies to add additional sleeping accommodations at the base camp. The three of us headed off into the quiet and beauty of Yellowstone National Park. I began to appreciate the remoteness of this park. We were the only people after an hour and a half of traveling at 25 miles per hour through vague snowy outlines of roads, often making our own trail.

Base camp occupied a unique location in the heart of Yellowstone—a small meadow surrounded by pine forest a half-mile from the majestic Grand Canyon Falls on the Yellowstone River. The roar of water constantly filled our ears as it crashed down 109 feet as it raced toward the Lower Falls for another 308-foot drop.

The snow that mid-December lay 40 inches deep, and temperatures ranged from 20 on sunny days to 5 below zero at night. The air was crisp, clear, and invigorating. Once Arden positioned the Sno-Coach for unloading, we made our way down a previously shoveled path into his camp. The

propane-heated, canvas Quonset huts were arranged in a semi-circle on the packed snow. In the center stood a single circular canvas yurt that provided space for cooking, family-style eating, and all après ski entertainment. Inside each hut sat two narrow beds with just enough space to stand up and change clothes. We worked to put up another yurt, and an additional hut.

When those tasks were completed, Arden invited us to take an afternoon ski with him. From camp, we skied across the meadows of Cascade Creek and along the rim of the Grand Canyon of Yellowstone. Our first trek brought us to a stand of forest with trees still black from the historic fires of 1988, when over a third of the Park burned. We skied through a landscape of stark vertical black lines against a field of white, and it felt as if we were entering a black and white photograph.

Ginger and I were still getting our ski legs. We were a bit shaky on downhill descents, where we frantically grabbed onto the sooty trees to aid us in braking. Our jackets were soon smudged black. On the far side of the forest, we entered a meadow where a herd of bison lay in the afternoon sun. Miniature snowballs clung to their winter manes. I noticed a huge male nestled under a tree about 50 yards away. As if in a movie where the camera suddenly zooms in on the massive head of the animal, I experienced being one with this magnificent beast, as well as being physically small in comparison. Yet, I felt safe, and had an overwhelming certainty that all was well in the world—an experience unlike any I'd had before. The big fellow sensed my admiration. He hoisted his bulky body to a standing position, sinking up to his belly in snow. Then he used a combination of his enormous

hoofs and sense of smell to dig through the snow. Dig. Sniff. Dig, dig. Sniff. Then with one grand effort he scratched at the tundra to loosen the frozen grass. So much work for so little.

The sun was getting low, and we still had work to do. We skied back to camp with little conversation, still cherishing the magic moments of nature. The only thing that broke our silence was the sound of skis gliding through the snow.

"I've never felt so exhausted and exuberant at the same time!" I said as we clicked out of our ski bindings.

"Hey Arden, what's in that food box?" Ginger asked.

"Anything that will hit the spot?"

"It just so happens that I have steaks marinating for this occasion," he said.

"Yep, that will certainly hit the spot," we chimed in unison and hung our clothes on the inside line to dry. We pitched in with dinner prep of roasted potatoes, veggies, and steak. The meal was a perfect ending to our day in Yellowstone.

It was only a couple of hours to the airport in Bozeman. Since Arden was still deep in preparation for the incoming guests, I drove Ginger to the airport.

"Are you sure I can't convince you to stay?" I asked as we passed Big Sky Ski Area.

"Look Helen. You and Arden have things under control, and there isn't room for me at camp anyway, so just relax."

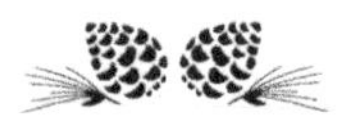

"I know. I know. It's going to be a super tough job spending a week in Yellowstone," I said, "but I guess someone has to do it!"

At the airport we hugged and said our good-byes. Arden had given me a shopping list. I crossed the items off, and with a well-stocked car, headed back. Two enthusiastic couples greeted me, the 'advance team' for the rest of the group, and we had a grand night of merriment as I listened to stories of their previous visit, and heard their dreams for the upcoming one. Three other couples arrived in the morning.

Nothing could have prepared me for the solitude and bliss I encountered in Yellowstone that week. Our first destination after arriving back at camp with the group was to visit the Grand Canyon Falls. Arden asked me to take the group out, as he had some work to do at camp.

"Um, I've skied in Yellowstone a grand total of twice, and that was only a couple of days ago," I said with panic in my voice.

"Don't worry," he said. "I've cut the trails. Just follow the signs, and you'll be fine. I'll join you in an hour."

"Well, okay," I said and turned to lead the group.

Some of the veterans had struck out on their own. The remaining four were novice skiers still struggling with their equipment. I got on my skis and began to follow Arden's trails to Inspiration Point, a seemingly fitting place for which to aim. Our first view of the falls that created the constant roar at camp was magnificent. Then someone in our group suggested we discard our skis in favor of trudging through the snow that blanketed the steps down to another landing, which offered an even more a perfect-picture taking opportunity of

the falls. It took us an hour to wade through thigh-high snow. We stopped midway totally winded.

"Maybe we should go back," I suggested, but the pull of the falls was too great for the group to give up and turn around. We fought on, and finally had the joy of snapping that perfect snow- and ice-covered waterfall shot. By the time we struggled back up to the trailhead, Arden was watching with amused curiosity.

"That was some hike you undertook," he said in a quizzical tone.

"Don't you admire our persistence? We were inspired." I said with a smile.

"I do have snowshoes at camp. Next time, take those instead of getting all wet in deep snow."

"I'll remember that, believe me."

Then he asked the group, "Do you want to go back or continue until sundown?"

There was a chorus. "We want to ski! That's why we're here."

Arden took us to one of his favorite places—an area of thermal hot springs, called the Norris Geyser Basin. We started in knee-deep snow, but within five minutes the snow grew heavy with moisture and stuck to the bottom of our skis. A few yards farther on, the depth of snow was only ankle deep. The air temperature grew spring-like, and we took off our skis and layers of clothing. Arden donned his geologist hat as he guided us around the delicate landscape with its mounds of earth of various sizes, colors—bright green, yellow, orange, — and sulfur-like smells.

We skied on toward the steaming haze rising off the river that meanders through Yellowstone and then heard a sound like no other! We soon caught our first glimpse of North America's largest waterfowl—the rare Trumpeter Swans. They weigh up to 30 pounds and have a wingspan of eight feet. I stood transfixed, thinking these beings were the most graceful and beautiful birds I'd ever seen. We whispered as if we were in church as we observed them. For a few moments, time stood still, and we experienced a majestic sense of well-being.

Another sacred time in Yellowstone was my first moonlight cross-country ski. The calmness of the night, the crispness of cold air moving in and out of my lungs, the long, blue shadows defining a landscape lit only by the moon, and a high dome of brilliant stars as I kicked and glided across sparkling snow, remain vivid in my mind to this day.

I understand why people return to Yellowstone year after year. When I was younger, I had envisioned a place like it, but for all of the breathtaking, awe-inspiring essence I imagined, I did not dream big enough.

Here I am with Yellowstone Falls
in the background © 1989

·2·

Canada

After a glorious week of cross-country skiing and rejuvenation in the canyon country of Yellowstone, it was time to close down camp, pack up gear, and head back to West Yellowstone.

The next day during down time at Arden's house, I noticed that he was busy filling out an application. When I asked, he told me that he was applying for a seasonal ranger position in Yellowstone, as it is the Park Service's procedure to have rangers apply for their position every year.

He handed me an extra application he happened to have. "Here, why don't you fill one of these out? You've got nothing to lose."

Inspired by the beauty out the window over his table, I sat down and began to answer ten pages of questions. Since I was a neophyte in the Federal employment process, it never occurred to me that people hone their resumes and fluff up their qualifications to secure the much-desired ranger positions.

The process was daunting and took the better part of an afternoon. The seasonal application covered a diverse array of skills, ranging from working with the public to operating a chain saw. It used a rating system scaled from one to five, with one being the lowest and five the highest; anything above a two required substantiation—either education or practical work experience. I had never seen such a detailed application for a three-month job.

I selected two parks I'd never heard of as first on my list of desired locations, thinking it would up my chance at success. It was early January, and the job wasn't to start for another six months.

"Here goes nothing," I said to myself as I dropped the application in the mail the next day. After that I never gave it another thought.

Ginger flew in from Seattle. There was so much to share about my time in Yellowstone. I was a torn between hoping her visit had gone well and wanting it to fall short of her expectations, so that I wouldn't lose a travel partner.

I met her at the gate with a big hug. "Welcome back! Did you have a good time?"

"Yes, it was fine."

"Only fine?"

"Yeah."

"Well, are you happy to be back on the road?"

"Yes—and no."

I felt an emotional cloud settle over us as we walked toward the car.

“What do you mean—yes and no?”

"No, I miss Keith," she said, “and yes, I'm happy to be back with you on our big adventure."

"I have loads to tell you about Yellowstone." We had a couple of nights of catching up as we planned the next leg of our trek.

I noticed that Ginger's spirits began to lift as we repacked the car, excited to embark on the next leg of our journey. Since we were close to Canada, we couldn't pass up the opportunity. We bid Arden farewell, pointed the car north,

and set our sights on Banff, knowing we could and would give in to our whims at any moment along the way.

We were committed to reaching Canada by nightfall. This meant we had to drive through the Blackfoot Indian Reservation that stands between Helena, Montana and the border. It was dusk by the time we reached the signs saying we were entering the Reservation. There were several abandoned single-story houses in various stages of decay, unkempt yards with tufts of crab grass, a lonely, paint-peeling motel, and a strange absence of people. The stark, dismal surroundings set our nerves on edge. The prospect of miles of nothing but barren landscape was alarming. There were no support services to be seen. I pulled over ready, to turn around.

"Don't stop. We've got to keep going," Ginger said with a worried look.

On the straight road I speeded up. We had no desire to spend the night in a scary, unknown place where white women might be at a distinct disadvantage. Miles farther north, we kept reassuring each other of our decision, in spite of our doubts. The car sped on in the growing dark through the lonely heart of the reservation, over hilly roads and hairpin curves.

At 6 p.m., we breathed a sigh of relief as the border station finally came into view. We slowed; the headlights illuminated a sign: "Border Crossing Closed 5 p.m. to 7 a.m."

"Oh no," I moaned, "who ever heard of the Canadian border closing? I lived within 20 miles of Canada most of my life, and never once was the border closed."

We sat in the car staring at the sign. Every choice seemed equally unappealing. Should we pull over, lock the

doors, get out the sleeping bags, and curl up in the car? Should we drive on the lonely roads to the only motel we'd seen on the reservation many miles back—a rundown, unappealing place where it looked as if rooms were rented by the hour? It was probably the only resting place within 75 miles. Neither of us relished the thought of shivering in a cold car all night, so we headed back into the dark of the reservation for the motel.

When we pulled into the parking lot, we sat in the car for several minutes working up enough nerve to go in.

"Well, I see a small light in the corner room," I said. "Guess that's the office. Let's go."

"Who said anything about 'we'?" Ginger replied.

"Don't you dare chicken out on me now. We're in this together."

"Well, if there's someone in there with a gun, one of us needs to survive to call the police," Ginger said. I opened her door.

We grabbed our jackets, stepped out of the car, and headed toward the light. We were immediately greeted by a thick cloud of old cigarette smoke. A small desk lamp sat atop a high counter, and faded blue walls still held promise of days gone by. A plump old man grunted at the interruption to a TV program our arrival had caused.

"Uh, good evening sir. Do you have any rooms?" I asked, hoping the answer would be no.

"Uh huh," came his monotone reply.

"And the room rate would be?"

The man was slow to answer. He looked us over as if to size us up for something. What that 'something' was, I wasn't willing to think about.

"Fifty dollars cash," came his reply.

Way steep, I thought, and glanced sideways at Ginger to see if we were thinking the same thing.

"How about $20?" I bargained.

"$40."

"$35. It's all we have."

"I'll take it."

Digging into my pocket, I produced the cash. The man handed us a key—room 10, second floor. Apparently, no registration was necessary. We walked up a creaking wooden staircase to the doorway with a roughly painted black 10. Curtains half hung in the double window, allowing us a glimpse into the room. I jiggled the key, grateful at least it wasn't room 13, then took a deep breath and unlocked the door. It swung in and I felt the wall beside the door for a switch. There was none.

After stumbling around, we found a small lamp on a beat-up nightstand between two saggy beds. Wallpaper that had long lost its glue was peeling above the headboards. The carpet was thread-bare and stained from years of use.

"I should have held out for $20," I said.

"At least it's warm." Ginger was ever the optimist.

"Yup, you're right. It's warm."

We dropped our gear onto our respective beds.

"Which one of us is brave enough to check out the bathroom?" I rolled my eyes.

We rounded the corner expecting the worst and weren't disappointed. The toilet and tub were stained brown from rusty water, but we were lucky enough to have toilet paper and a smoky mirror. After the bathroom inspection, we were startled by a loud bang from a nearby room.

"Please tell me that wasn't gunshot," I said.

"No, it sounded more like our neighbors are having a little rough sex play." Ginger giggled.

After unpacking our sleeping bags, we made plans to bolt at daybreak. We nestled in as best we could, given our state of paranoia. There were sounds of dogs barking, running footsteps, loud cars, shouting, and other more suspicious noises. Finally, out of pure exhaustion, we fell asleep. Up with daylight, we packed as fast as we could, shoveled in Cheerios and milk, jumped into the car, and drove straight to the border.

At the crossing, I fully expected to be waved through, as often happened at Canadian border crossings in New York, but the agent leaned out and motioned the car over, indicating we would be detained for questioning. We stood nervously at the high counter. Questions flew at us. How long are you going to be in Canada? What is the purpose of your visit? Show us how much money you have with you. Do you have means of securing more money while in the country? Apparently, this isolated outpost didn't receive a lot of traffic, and we were the lucky ones to help fill certain quotas. Once we had satisfied their demands, we asked if they would stamp the passports we were carrying in case our adventure took us into Mexico. They happily agreed, and we were on our way north once again.

Miles up the road, we passed an odd sign.

"What in the world was that?" I asked.

Ginger craned her neck around. "I can't believe it but I think it said Head Smashed-In Buffalo Jump."

"Huh? How could anyone come up with such a crazy name?" I pulled over. "Let's go see."

Sure enough, Head Smashed-In Buffalo Jump was in a location where the foothills of the Rocky Mountains meet the Great Plains. The sign said that the Jump bears witness to a method of hunting practiced by native people of the North American plains for 6,000 years. Due to their excellent understanding of the regional topography and of bison behavior, native people often hunted the animals by stampeding them over a precipice. They then carved up the carcasses, dragged the pieces to be butchered and processed in a camp set up on the flats beyond the cliffs.

This isolated place in the middle of the prairie received its name because during one hunt, a young brave wanted to watch from the downside of the cliff as the buffalos fell onto the prairie below. The hunt that year was particularly good, and the brave was buried in buffaloes, his head smashed due to the weight of the animals and his proximity to the cliff wall. In 1981 it became an UNESCO world heritage site, a remarkable place with a matter-of-fact name.

We spent our first night in Calgary, home of the 1988 Winter Olympics. Vestiges of Olympic venues were still active throughout the city, such as the visitor center, bobsled run, and ice rinks. I was enthralled with the fact that so many people were friendly and spoke English. I'd grown up on the Quebec border. It had never occurred to me that people in the rest of Canada generally spoke English. We had a fun time checking out the local watering holes and enjoying the hospitality of Calgarians.

Banff, nestled in the beautiful Canadian Rockies, was a short drive from Calgary, heading due west on the Trans-Canada Highway. It catered to youthful travelers, having recently built a new hostel located in perfect proximity to Lake Louise and the ski area. At the hostel, we met people from all over the world. Wendy, a 19-year-old girl from Australia, was backpacking around the world for a year by herself. We were impressed with such an ambitious endeavor and asked what countries she was planning to visit.

"Canada, England, Egypt, and India." she replied without hesitation.

"What? No United States?"

"There's so much I want to see in the States, I don't think I'll have time," she said. We adopted her and, for a few weeks, our travel duo became a trio.

Our first expedition together was a recommended area for cross-country skiing at Moosequito Creek north of Banff. We stayed at a primitive outpost extension of the youth hostel—four small cabins with wood stoves and no running water, indoor plumbing, or electricity. The water source was a stream that ran alongside the cabins and required breaking through three inches of ice to lower the bucket. Lucky for us it had a wood-heated sauna.

We had the place mostly to ourselves. After a long day of backcountry skiing, we returned to our cabin just before sundown in order to prep for dinner and get the wood sauna stoked.

By the time we finished our gas lamp dinner, the stars had come out and the black of night enveloped us. We tested the sauna and decided that the heat had worked itself to the

proper level. Imagine our surprise to discover there was a strange man sitting in the dark corner of the warm room, but since it was a communal sauna, we proceeded with our original plan.

I had never experienced a Finnish Sauna before and was intrigued by the concept, although I was usually demure about exposing my naked body. That night I allowed myself freedom to trust my travel companions. We stripped off our clothes in the small outside room, then closed the sauna door behind us, lost in the heat and absolute darkness. I felt my way around the bench, got comfortable on the wooden plank seat, and granted myself the liberty of the experience without reservation. After 15 minutes of sweaty bliss, my solitude was abruptly interrupted. Was that someone inching over close to me on the bench? I slid over a few inches. Then a strange hand touched my thigh. Alarmed, I forcefully shoved the hand away, only to have it move to my breast! In the pitch black I calculated where the strange man's face would be and slapped it. There was a collective gasp. In a flash the door flew open exposing two moons as he ran out.

"What was that about?" asked Ginger

"The jerk was feeling me up," I answered, still alarmed and disgusted.

Wendy laughed. "He certainly made the rounds. He tried the same thing with me and apparently kept working the room when I rejected him. Good job, Helen!"

"That is so utterly disturbing," I said.

"Well, let's forget about that pervert and get back to sweating," Ginger said.

After 20 more minutes of extreme moist heat, we bucked up enough courage to step outside and roll in the

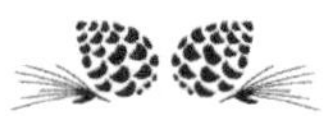

snow. Never had I been so exhilarated. I understood for the first time why going to extremes is often beneficial to life.

Wendy (on left) & I at Moosequito Creek © 1989

·3·

The Drunken Line Continues

It had always been our intention to hop from one ski area to another, so for the next three months, Ginger and I zigzagged our way down the Rockies. One of our target areas was Whitefish, Montana, located about 50 miles from the Canadian border and a natural next stop.

Our only lead for free housing in Whitefish was to look up a guy I had met months before at a friend's wedding. I remembered the night vividly. Scott had offered to give me a ride back to my hotel after the reception. Being naive, I agreed, only to find a rather rambunctious, inebriated man, eager for a one-night stand. I wasn't emotionally ready for that, so the evening ended with a brief kiss and nothing more. I was unsure of how I would be greeted after my refusal of his advances, but in the interest of cheap lodging, I cast uneasiness aside and decided to track him down.

The information I had was that Scott was tending bar at a ski area in Whitefish. Luckily for us, there was only one ski area, so we did the logical thing. After a fantastic day of skiing, we enjoyed a hot toddy, and sure enough, behind the bar stood Scott.

"Hi Scott," I said, and in an effort to refresh his memory, "I'm Helen. We met at Lynn and Dan's wedding, remember?"

After a blank look, he said, "Oh—hi."

I was disappointed. Apparently the lost one-night stand was forgotten—or not so memorable.

"Lynn told me you made your way out west and encouraged me to look you up if I was in the area. Obviously, I'm in the area. This is my friend, Ginger. We were hoping to impose on your hospitality for a couple of days."

Scott smiled. What did that smile mean? That he was going to have two ladies to score with? That he would enjoy the company?

"Sure," he said. "It would be fun. I'm staying with my brother, and he's in Utah for the next week, so I have a big empty house. You'd have to leave before he comes back."

We happily agreed to leave before his brother's arrival. We would have been satisfied with a hot shower and enough floor space for sleeping bags. As it turned out, our accommodations were swanky. It was an exquisite, three-bedroom log cabin on the outskirts of town that looked like something out of Architectural Digest—carefully chosen light fixtures, earth toned furnishings, hardwood floors, and a grand stone fireplace.

Ginger and I happily offered our cooking and cleaning skills and tried to be the perfect houseguests for a young bachelor.

Whitefish exceeded all expectations. The skiing was sublime. The week flew by—good food, great conversation, new friends. We were surprised when an unexpected truck drove up the driveway several nights later.

Scott jumped up and shouted, "Oh no. It's my brother!"

We froze, fearing that we would be instantly shoved out into the cold. Scott explained our presence to his brother who offered a broad warm smile and plopped himself on the

couch extending his legs onto the coffee table. "Do you have to go tomorrow? Why not stay longer?"

With a sigh of relief, we all opened another beer, and the merriment continued.

The next morning, we cooked a hardy breakfast for the guys, repacked the car, and said our good-byes. There were other adventures waiting.

I left Whitefish feeling anxious, as it was time for Ginger to visit her boyfriend, Keith, in Washington state—again. This seemed to be getting a little too serious for my comfort.

"I know we've planned this for a while, but I'll feel lost without you," I said, as we drove to the airport in Bozeman—again. "I can't help but feel jealous. You're going to Seattle, and you have someone who loves you waiting for you there."

"Well, Helcat, I'll be back before you know it, and we'll pick up where we left off." Ginger seemed oblivious to my feelings of inadequacy.

We had become lifelong friends in a few short weeks. I loved her company and enjoyed her extroverted personality. She was often the catalyst for our meeting new people. Without the safety net that Ginger frequently provided, I feared that I'd be stretched out of my social comfort zone. The thought of her leaving again was unnerving, but what was I to do? I dropped Ginger off with a hug at the airport.

The drive to Jackson Hole was one of those unexpected pleasures that were always cropping up in the Rockies. The aptly named Grand Tetons provided a

breathtaking backdrop to the big western sky. I was alone on the road and found myself enjoying the solitude. The drive allowed time to reflect on the events of the past few weeks.

"I wonder what interesting experiences await me all by myself?" I asked aloud as I drove into Jackson Hole. After a brief drive around town, I knew that I wasn't going to ski there. I was surprised at my disappointment. Jackson Hole reminded me of a Disney version of a western town—lovely, but fake at the same time.

"I guess Salt Lake City is where I'm meant to be tonight," I said, and turned the car around.

In Salt Lake City, I managed to find the hostel which was located in a part of town that was on the other side of the proverbial tracks. I was tired from the long day's drive and feeling shy. I sat in the common room, making no attempt at conversation. A man approached me with a warm smile.

"Hi, I'm Michael Walker."

I noted his Australian accent. "Hi. I'm Helen."

"What areas are you planning to ski?" he asked.

"I'm not sure. I've read about so many, it's hard to choose. But I'm open to recommendations."

"One of my favorites is Alta. I'm skiing there tomorrow. Would you like to go?"

"Well, I must warn you that I'm a novice. I'm afraid I would slow you down."

"Don't worry about that, mate. We'll have a good day."

I took a deep breath and overcame my nervousness. "Okay, then."

"Great! You won't be disappointed. It's the best snow I've ever skied on. What time shall we meet?"

"You tell me, and I'll be ready. I'm happy to drive."

"Let's meet at 7:30. That'll give us time to have breakfast, drive to the mountain, and be at the summit for first run by 10."

Michael did not exaggerate the amazing conditions at the mountain. As I suspected, I was a complete novice compared to him. He was a powder-hound, and I was happy to stay on groomed trails. He patiently waited as I meandered my way down a run, then at the bottom encouraged me to try a run through the trees. I was terrified at the prospect, but committed to advancing my skills, I agreed.

"I don't want to hold you up. You go first, and I'll follow," I said.

"Are you sure? I don't want to leave you."

"Don't worry. I'll be right behind you. I promise."

He turned his skis downhill and vanished into the trees. I could see him hopping like a jackrabbit, looking completely at ease as he swished through the woods. I was anything but relaxed. The whole point of skiing in the trees was to experience the fluffy powder. I quickly discovered that skiing in deep powder requires a completely different technique than skiing on groomed trails. One has to sit back on the skis in order for the tips to glide up through the snow and not be pulled down into it. It was a delicate balance between sitting back enough and leaning forward to keep the momentum.

It felt awkward. I could hardly keep my balance as trees flew by. My heart was in my mouth; breathing was a challenge; I wanted to scream. Survival was the only thought that raced through my mind as I narrowly missed tree after

tree. Michael had made it look so easy. I leaned to the right, caught a glimpse of the trail, and prayed my luck would hold in dodging the trees. I felt faint as I made it to the groomed trail where he was waiting.

"Well. How'd you like it?" he asked.

I tried to hide my shaking body. "Um, after I got through my initial panic about being wrapped around a tree, I-I guess it was exhilarating."

"Want to go again?" he asked.

"No thank you. Go enjoy. I'll stick to the groomed trails."

He made the next couple of runs through the trees, while I explored the rest of what the mountain had to offer. By late afternoon, my legs were jelly, and I was ready to get out of my ski boots and relax. However, we were surprised to find the lodge filled beyond capacity.

"Would you like to have dinner in town?" Michael asked.

"Oh, I thought you'd be tired of me by now," I said, then felt stupid and clumsy, but the prospect of dinner with an attractive and interesting person was appealing.

"No, the skiing was fun. Now we get to the interesting part."

My face must have flushed as he looked intently into my eyes and smiled. I looked away to give myself time to regain composure.

"What interesting part?" I heard myself ask. My voice sounded defensive, maybe confrontational. I scrambled to recall any hints from our day. Our conversations during the lift rides were plutonic, free-flowing. I didn't think there were any sexual undertones. Had I missed some cues or clues? It

wouldn't be the first time I'd misread a situation. Had I not been 'interesting' all day?

"Well, things like why does a woman travel alone to ski and what, besides skiing, does she do for fun?"

"Oh, I was so intent on skiing, I guess I forgot to cover the basics. I would like to have dinner in town. We can talk more then," I said in an attempt to change the subject.

"There's an inexpensive Chinese restaurant near the hostel," he suggested.

"Great. I like Chinese food, and it sounds like the price is right." We got into my car for the drive to town. "Thanks for encouraging me," I said. "The area certainly lived up to your advertising. How long are you planning to stay?"

"Through the rest of the season. I can't imagine any better conditions. You?"

"I'm heading out tomorrow. I have friends and relatives in Denver and Colorado Springs."

We decided to go straight to dinner without bothering to change out of our ski gear. The restaurant had a warm welcoming atmosphere. The tables were decorated with little flower vases and tea candles. We seated ourselves in the corner and placed our order.

I tried to work up my courage and bring intentions out in the open. "Forgive me for being so bold, but did I miss something in the invitation to skiing and dinner?"

"I'm not sure I know what you mean," he said, but I saw worry in his eyes.

"I guess what I'm trying to say are you expecting anything other than casual conversation and a good meal?"

He sat for a moment and chewed on his lower lip. I began to feel very foolish.

After what seemed a long time, he said, "Well, that would be a very lovely offer if there was something more you were willing to do. However, it would be lost on me. My attraction lies with men."

I looked down embarrassed. "Oh. I-I'm really sorry if I misread your comments." Then I sighed with relief. "I wasn't meaning to offer anything. I thought our day was quite friendly. Then you made that comment about things becoming 'interesting'. I can be unbelievably thick. Seems most of my gay friends prefer sand and surf, instead of slopes and sun. Apparently, you're not typical."

He laughed. "I've made it a practice to be a bit guarded. I thought you would be safe. Skiing is my first love, and it's always wonderful to share it. I was right; you are safe *and* a pleasure to be with. You'll make someone a wonderful partner someday, Helen. Is there a someone? I gather not, because you're traveling by yourself. Are you looking?"

Now it was my turn to delay response. Clearly Michael was someone I could trust. After dinner I would never see him again, so what did I have to lose? You could lose the pretense of believing that you have the whole relationship thing figured, I thought. When you pretend for a really long time, that's just the way life becomes. And you kind of forget you made it up. But admitting the problematic truth was hard, so I stuck with the old story.

"I'm not sure I'm looking for a relationship actually," I said struggling to sound confident. I was remembering how painful it was for me when my parents divorced. I was away at school, and for some reason I found myself caught in the

middle of their struggle. Each wanted to express their reasoning or misery during the phone conversations I had with them. "I guess I've drawn some conclusions through my observation of relationships over the years."

"Oh, what are they?"

"Conclusion number one: relationships can be painful emotionally and physically. Number two: there are just too many compromises, and you don't get to do what you really want to do. Number three: relationships end, so hey, why bother? In a nutshell, there's way too much to figure out first."

"Fair enough," he said, and smiled a knowing smile. "I'm sure you'll have one when you do figure it out."

I spent several weeks in Colorado after that, enjoying free lodging and skiing expertise offered by my college friend, Kim. Then Kim and I met Ginger at the Denver airport, and we reviewed our laundry list of places we still wanted to ski. Kim introduced us to some of the lesser known, but still incredibly awesome, areas. It's always a treat to ski with the locals, as tourist areas tend to get out of hand. We were challenged by the trails at Berthoud Pass, which was the last vestige of Wild West skiing. Only the hardy skier could enjoy the un-groomed and unmarked trails, while allowing the pokiness of a single lift "drop you at the top" so you can do it all over again. We enjoyed the variety and layout of Copper Mountain; cherished the remoteness of Monarch. We were blown by as if we were standing still by a blind skier and her guide in Winter Park, where they had a wonderful Assisted Ski Program.

It was mid-March already when we started to make our way south toward New Mexico to take in Taos before they closed for the season. En route, we had enough time to swing into Telluride. The date just happened to be March 17, exactly one year since Ginger and I had met for the first time. We thought it fitting to celebrate with a bodacious day of skiing in a historic town. It seemed like the Universe was on board. We were delighted to discover hang gliders taking off from the summit, splashing the sky with vibrant blue, green, orange, and yellow. We were thrilled with the warm weather and cast aside our winter parkas for sweatshirts. The town of Telluride was prepared for their annual St. Patrick's Day celebration. Wearing o' the green, corned beef and cabbage dinners, and free flowing taps were plentiful. Ginger and I were happy to punctuate a day of superlative skiing with a good meal and a couple of beers.

We studied the map that night and decided to visit Mesa Verde National Monument and stop at highlights along the way, such as Durango. We got a late start the next day, due to an impromptu hike, and found ourselves in Silverton too tired to drive to Durango. The town was an unexpected gold (and silver) mine of history and charm! The historic Grand Hotel doubled as a hostel. Besides the participants of a fencing tournament, Ginger and I almost had the place to ourselves.

"Hey Ginge," I whispered down from the top bunk that night.

"Yeah?"

"I've been meaning to ask—what's the deal with you and Keith?"

"Well, you know we were dating last summer, right?"

"Yeah. I kinda guessed these trips to Seattle were more than social visits."

"I went to meet his parents."

"Wow. That sounds serious."

"Well, he did ask me to marry him."

"WHAT?" I yelled and immediately covered my mouth, as I remembered the thin hostel walls. "When?" I whispered.

"He asked before I left on this trip."

I was astonished. "And you still came?"

Well, I told him this trip was something I really had to do and that I'd give consideration to his proposal while I was traveling."

"Wow, talk about an understanding guy, huh."

She laughed, and we didn't speak for a few minutes, both of us lost in thought.

"Ginge?" I said breaking the silence. "I never told you about the guy I met in Utah. His name was Michael."

"Oh, this is juicy! I'm all ears."

"Sorry to spoil the punch line, but nothing happened. We had a great day of skiing and then dinner." I filled her in on the details of our dinner conversation.

"So, why did you bring it up?" she asked.

"I don't know. Maybe I'm beginning to think one of the reasons I'm on this trip is to figure out the big question of my life."

"Which is?"

I shrugged and sighed. "I guess whether to be in a relationship or not."

"And why would you not want to find a boyfriend? I mean no real hurry, but you know, you are twenty-seven."

I looked down and bit my lip; a sense of desperation bordering on panic began to rise. I noticed she had substituted 'boyfriend' for relationship. Was that uncomfortable? "Um. Well. The truth is I never dated in high school—or college either."

I imagined amazement on Ginger's face, but she didn't say a word.

"Well, you know, I've had plenty of guy friends," I hurried to assure her. "I used to do lots of fun-type things with them, but I guess I never quite had the confidence to actually date."

"Why not?" she asked.

"I think I'm petrified to allow myself to be open and vulnerable. How can I be with someone when I haven't sorted out things for myself?"

"Well, maybe you don't have to sort them out all by your lonesome. I'm here for you, and I'll love you no matter what you decide," Ginger said in a delicate tone. Then she leaned over to smile up at me with encouragement on her face.

"Thanks. That means a lot to me that I can open the door a little and trust you. But you know how I always want to do everything myself. I've had years of guarding myself, only letting people in so far. It always seemed so risky. I like to show people the fun, confident side of me. Exposing something more scares the hell out of me."

"It's always risky, Helcat. I'll let you in on a little secret—you're more transparent than you know. Don't think I haven't noticed after all these months of travelling that there's more to you than the fun, affable, independent girl. You know

what I'm thinking? It's good to finally begin to see the whole Helen. What is normal anyway these days? We're not normal; the two of us traveling around together like this. Maybe you should ask yourself what would happen if you took a risk. You might be surprised."

"Yeah, well maybe," I said with a yawn. "Thanks for listening. It doesn't seem quite so big and scary now."

"Anytime, Helcat. Anytime. G'night."

"G'night."

The next day we reached Mesa Verde National Park by mid-morning. Yellowstone had been my introduction to National Parks, but it was Mesa Verde that opened my eyes to the world of ancient culture and interpretative rangers. There was a familiarity about the place that I couldn't explain. I felt connected at a level I had never known existed. The ranger donned her cool hat, and we set out on a semi-personal tour of the Spruce Tree House.

We climbed down a steep winding path that descended 100 feet to the stone ruins set in an alcove below a giant overhanging cliff. Due to the protection of the overhang, this dwelling had very little deterioration. It had the remains of over 130 rooms and eight kivas, or round ceremonial chambers, all made of meticulously chosen stone from the mesa above. While some walls towered 30 feet above us, the kivas descended 20 feet into the ground. They were circular, in stark juxtaposition to the straight, square walls of the joined rooms. I peered down into one kiva and saw the stone benches lining the wall, with circular room for about 20 people. This is a place I have been, I thought, a location of great importance for seasonal community gatherings and close

to our rooms. We entered a nearby room through a T-shaped door, and it was as if a portal had opened through which I stepped.

My imagination took over as the ranger told the story of the ancient Anasazi, the ancestral Pueblo dwellers in New Mexico. These people flourished for over 700 years before the Europeans set foot on North America. They built elaborate communities in the sheltered alcoves of canyon walls. At the bottom of the canyons and up on the mesas above they kept gardens of beans and corn and supplemented their diet by hunting game.

We walked from one ruin to another. I saw myself performing everyday work and climbing up the vertical canyon wall via the carved hand-and-foot holds in the rock. When I reached the top, I joined my neighbors in harvesting corn from the mesa. We worked in unison to lower the abundance down to the village below, using a rope and basket system. Several of us stayed on the mesa filling the baskets, while the rest would climb below ready to receive corn as it was lowered. It was essential to get the corn dried on the roof of our house before winter, and I remembered watching the storm clouds gathering behind me and working very fast. Later in the fall, young girls would get to sit together and laugh and trade stories while grinding corn for their mothers to make into life sustaining food all winter.

Why did this place feel so oddly real? I kept my observations to myself as I listened, aware that my senses were being overwhelmed with memories. I could see the ranger talking and gesturing, but barely understood the words as I pictured the Ancient Ones—and no, I hadn't smoked peyote before entering the site!

"You were way quiet up there, Helcat. Everything all right?" Ginger asked as we drove away.

I nodded. "I had a strange experience out there," I finally said. "I felt this incredible connection to that place. It was as if my mind was split in two; as if I had these clear memories of living there while the ranger was talking about living there. I even wanted to say once, no, no, it wasn't quite like that. Weird, huh. I'm just trying to process it."

Some miles later Ginger looked up from her knitting and said, "I thought it was awesome that there was a female park ranger. She really seemed to know her stuff."

"Yeah. It sure seems like a fun job."

·4·

The Offer

"Hi Mom."

"Hi Sweetie. How are you?"

"Oh, I'm fine."

"Where are you?"

"We're at a youth hostel in Taos getting ready for our last day of skiing. You won't believe it, but it's an absolutely beautiful spring day out here—70 degrees and sunny. Perfect to be on the slopes. So hey, what's happening in New York?"

"Oh, things are fine. It's 42 degrees, cloudy, and it snowed again yesterday. You know the story. By the way, you got a call from some guy named Dan Hand."

I frowned. "From where?"

"I'm not sure—a park out west I think."

"Oh my God! I almost forgot. Way back in January I applied to be a ranger at a couple of parks, but I don't even remember where now. Wow, you're kidding! What did he want?"

"He wants to talk with you about a job."

Mothers always want you to have a job. Even though mine knew I was completely happy living the nomadic life, she did her duty and pressed me to follow up. I scribbled down the number and promised I'd call him.

The next day, I reached Dan Hand, the hiring manager for the interpretive division of Glen Canyon National Recreation Area. I asked him to explain exactly where Glen

Canyon was located and confessed that although I remembered applying, I had forgotten which parks I had indicated interest. My strategy had been to list two parks that I'd never heard of, because I figured everyone would want to work in Yosemite, Grand Canyon, and Yellowstone. It seemed that my strategy had worked!

Dan explained that Glen Canyon is on the border of Utah and Arizona. The job would include working at the visitor center, developing interpretive talks about the area, hosting campfire programs, and working at a marina on Lake Powell. A lake in the desert? It sounded like a heavenly reprieve from the grueling restaurant work I had been relying on to survive, but there was one critical, deal-breaking question.

"Do I get to wear that neat hat?" I asked.

"Indeed, you do," Dan replied, and I could hear the smile in his voice. "Not only do you get to *wear* one, you will actually become the *owner* of one the moment you start work."

"Sounds like nirvana," I told him. "When do I start?"

We negotiated a date, as I had no interest in cutting short my already planned travelling schedule. Ginger and I still had several National Parks on our list, such as Arches, Bryce, Zion, and most of all, the Grand Canyon. But Glen Canyon was only a 300-mile detour from our next destination, so we decided to check it out.

We travelled southwest from Mesa Verde with a stop planned at the Four Corners. This attraction consisted of a concrete slab inlaid with perpendicular lines intersecting each other and the names of states on the respective slices of the

pie—Utah, Colorado, New Mexico and Arizona. The slab was surrounded by rows of haphazardly constructed, open wooden shanties with rusted corrugated metal roofs. Native Americans selling jewelry and stone carvings sat in the huts looking rather bored. The attraction was a letdown, but since we'd made the effort, we had our picture taken standing at the intersection, so we could prove we had been in four states at one time.

Only two roads led away from there. We decided to take the less travelled western road into Page, Arizona. Ginger consulted our trusty tourist guidebook.

"It says the town of Page was built as a housing camp to support the workers who constructed Glen Canyon Dam starting in 1957. Oh my God, Helcat, the dam is absolutely massive! Look at this picture. It's over 700 feet high. It says Lake Powell is the second largest artificial body of water in the country—hmm, and it's a popular houseboat and water-skiing area." She elbowed me. "Not too shabby, huh? Oh, but the Glenn Canyon Recreation Area gets over a million visitors each year. I guess you'll be super busy."

I was hardly listening to her chatter. It was the first time I had driven through real desert and my eastern prejudice expected dull sand as far as the eye could see, tumbleweed blowing against broken-down fences, flat, boring, and empty. Nothing in my life had prepared me for the cacophony of deep colors on display—iridescent reds, purples, oranges, yellows, tans, and browns—as if a grand artist had been whimsically at play, splashing the vista with a giant paintbrush. We drove through Monument Valley, where 500-foot high red sandstone monoliths stood sentinel, commanding our attention and signaling that we were entering a sacred place. I absorbed the

stunning magic, and during that drive, fell in love so deeply with the desert, that I thought I would never want to leave.

We passed through the Painted Desert and the endless Navajo Reservation and finally pulled into Page. My expectations weren't very high for a town that was only five years older than I was. It had a western feel and was built on a mesa overlooking the huge dam with a row of churches, stores, school, softball fields, and a robust strip mall with a grocery, Taco Bell, and two-screen movie theater. There were lots of adobe-colored ranch style houses, and dusty streets, reflecting the flatness of the arid surrounding desert. I was surprised to see tall cottonwood trees that provided much needed shade from the relentless sun. For a town of six thousand people that hosted a million visitors a year, it was remarkably clean, give or take a dust storm or two. Yes, this could work, I thought.

Most of Glen Canyon Recreation Area was located north of the dam in southeastern Utah along the shores of Lake Powell. We could smell the water as we drove over the Glen Canyon Bridge, the lifeline that links the Recreation Area with the town. When we stopped in the crowded parking lot, I looked at the map, amazed that over 200 miles and 1.2 million acres of land separated the Area's northern and southern ends.

A vista of red sandstone cliffs and beehive rock formations against the deep blue water of the lake stretched before us. The colossal white crescent of the concrete dam marked an abrupt interruption to the enchantment. Our first stop was the Visitor Center to meet Dan Hand, and lighten our load by dropping off my ski equipment. Dan was a career ranger whose endearing accent told me he had originated from somewhere south of the Mason-Dixon line. He had a pleasant,

relaxed demeanor, and I could tell I'd enjoy working with him and that he could teach me how to be a good interpretative ranger.

"I'm kind of apprehensive about this," I admitted. "I mean, I don't know exactly how to put together a campfire program."

"Not to worry," he assured me. "Interpretation is all about telling a story, whether it's through pictures, words, or song." Then, without hesitation and in the middle of the crowded Center, he broke into one of my favorite songs, all the while miming the characters. I laughed and joined in.

In a cabin in the wood,
Little old man by the window stood,
Saw a rabbit hopping by, frightened as can be.
"Help me! Help me! the rabbit said,
"Or the hunter'll shoot me dead!"
"Come little rabbit, come with me. Safe we will be."

"Don't worry, Helen," he assured me, "your first program won't be until later in the summer. We have plenty of time to work on it together. And by the way, singing is optional," he added with a mischievous smile.

I was relieved to know that I wouldn't have to break into song at any point in my employment. I stored my skis and followed Dan, as he gave us a tour of the circular visitor center poised on the edge of a sandstone cliff over the Colorado River. A large three-dimensional relief map of the immense Recreation Area occupied a huge space in the middle of the room. The semi-circle wall of floor-to-ceiling windows overlooked a glorious view of the dam, lake, and river that feeds the area. I walked over to stand next to the one of the

windows and gaze at the monstrously tall dam. With a thrill of both fear and anticipation, I thought, this is the perfect metaphor for going over the edge—and that's what I'm about to do.

Dan had provided instructions to the local campground near the marina on the lake that was located five miles north of the Visitor Center. Ginger and I set up our trusted orange, two-person tent. That night, as I lay in my sleeping bag wide-awake, thrills of excitement kept running through me. I listened to the cool wind ripple off the water and the slapping of rope on the houseboats moored nearby.

"I feel so blessed to have this amazing opportunity to live here," I said to Ginger as we lay side by side in our sleeping bags.

"Yep, you really bagged it this time, Helcat. I can't wait to hear how it goes."

"Are you planning to go be with Keith when we're done with our trip?"

"That will be a bit difficult. I'll be in L.A. and he's in Massachusetts."

"Oh, you mean that job came through?"

"Right. I'll probably fly out East a couple of times this summer."

"Ginge, promise me something."

"What?"

"Promise you won't marry him right away, okay? I think we still have a lot of travelling to do together."

"Look. No need to worry. I'm not ready to make that commitment yet."

I closed my eyes finally ready for sleep. Despite my uneasiness about the coming parting from Ginger, I knew that life couldn't get any better than this!

Image courtesy of the National Park Service

·5·

To the Bottom and Back Again

During the whole trip I had been eagerly looking forward to our ultimate destination—the Grand Canyon. Our planned four-day visit was the culmination hike of the grand adventure of friends that Ginger and I had enjoyed for six months.

Ginger had asked me a month before if she could invite Keith to hike with us and, in the spirit of cooperation, I agreed. I didn't realize the impact of making our month's-long duo a trio.

Now we had to take a side trip down to Phoenix to pick him up at the airport. It was a rather silent four-hour ride. Suddenly it felt to me as if *our* trip had just turned into *her* trip.

"I'll drive around and watch for you," I said dropping Ginger off curbside.

As I circled, I was grateful for the time alone. I needed an attitude adjustment if the last leg of our trip was going to be a success, but the best I could manage as I pulled up in front of the happy couple was a weak smile.

"Well, daylight is burning," I said, trying to be lighthearted, but knowing my voice sounded tight. "Let's load up and head to the canyon."

"I'll drive," Ginger offered. I shrugged, gave Keith the front seat and climbed into the back.

"Are you sure you want to sit back there?" he asked apologetically.

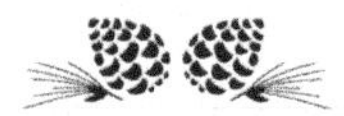

"Yeah. Why not?" I said. "You two catch up. Just pretend I'm not here." I settled against the car window with my pillow and closed my eyes. When I woke, we were pulling up to a rather fancy Flagstaff hotel.

"Helen, Keith and I are going to get a room for the night," Ginger said.

I hadn't thought much about the logistics of having a boyfriend along. Of course, it made sense that the two young lovers would want to be alone, but that thought didn't take the sting out of it for me. In reality, I would be the one who was alone. Ginger noticed the shock on my face. "Do you want me to see if they have two rooms available," she hurried to say.

"No. I really don't have enough money to get a hotel room. I'll find some place to camp tonight and pick you up in the morning," I said, fighting back tears as I climbed out of the backseat.

"We could have dinner together," she offered.

"No, I have to find a place so I'm not scrambling by nightfall. I'll pick you up at 7."

"Hey Helcat, don't be upset," she said with a worried look. "Please."

"It's okay. Just let me go. I'll be fine."

I drove around Flagstaff in a daze for a half hour, maybe hoping a campground would turn up on the city streets. I felt punch-drunk and lost. It was early evening when I got myself together and turned the car north toward the mountains. After twenty miles, I took a small deserted dirt road off to the right. It traversed some empty looking fields with a few cattle and mountains off in the distance. Must be part of the National Forest, I thought, and anyone could camp on National Forest land. After a mile of not seeing any dwellings or sign of life, I decided to pull off and spotted a place by a large rock within eyesight of the car to pitch the tent.

I stared at the jumbled mess in the back of the car feeling lethargic. Across the dusty sage of the field, I lugged tent, flashlight, sleeping bag and pillow, bedroll, change of clothes, water, sandwich. I pitched the tent like a pro and filled it with necessities as the sun was setting behind the mountains. Then I crawled in and sat cross-legged to eat a day-old sandwich. No doubt stars were coming out like a light show, but my mind was heavy as I tried to make sense of my runaway feelings.

"Okay, Helen, why are you so upset?" I asked myself out loud. I sat in silence picking dusty pieces of grass from other campsites off our tent floor. "Okay," I said, "okay, I admit, it's this damn relationship thing. It's confusing me again. If I keep saying I don't even want one, then why am I jealous when my friend has one? Huh? Why? Just deal with it, will you. And please get over it—now."

I figured there was nothing like being alone in the wilderness to take a long hard look at myself, so I lay down and stared up at the tent as it got dark, but my rebellious mind was blank. "Look," I finally said out loud, "if you can't trust yourself to answer this, then, who are you going to trust?"

I crawled into the sleeping bag in my clothes, since I'd forgotten to bring my pajamas, and the conversation with myself continued. "You're afraid to answer, aren't you? What is it that makes your mind like mush around this? Do you want a boyfriend, huh? Maybe you want a girlfriend, is

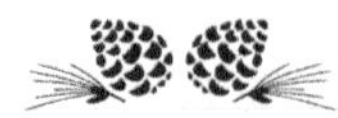

that it?" The naggy old question had surfaced again. "No, no, I assured myself, I am attracted to men. Well, I am, aren't I? Okay, I'm terrified."

For me the idea of having a boyfriend brought up old unwelcome feelings. What were they? Loneliness, inadequacy, isolation, fear. This was going nowhere fast. I fell into a restless sleep without reaching any conclusions.

Camping under the stars also meant waking up with the sun. After re-packing the car with some degree of neatness, I made it back to Flagstaff by 6. Too early to pick up the lovers, so I found a diner and lingered over breakfast, emotions still raw from the night before.

We arrived at the Grand Canyon trailhead by eight. Our backcountry permit outlined us hiking down the South Kaibab trail, spending the night at the Bright Angel campground near the Colorado River, and taking two days for our return trip to the South Rim up the Bright Angel trail with an overnight stop at Indian Gardens.

Once we had adjusted our heavy backpacks and started down the trail, I walked far ahead of my friends for several hours, only pausing long enough to catch them in my sight before moving on. The long hike to the bottom of the canyon turned out to be a way to work out my insecurities. With each step, I plunged deeper into an all too familiar raw emotional space of upset and anger that I thought I had buried long ago. I attempted to reconcile my feelings like an old bank statement of past circumstances, but still came up short. Something didn't add up. Here I was in the most beautiful place on the planet, and I didn't have the emotional stamina to take it in. It made me sadder than I'd ever been before. Then

a simple thought occurred to me—what if I was in this sacred canyon to *release* rather than take in?

I stopped in my tracks with the toes of my shoes hanging over the sharp edge of the trail. Ginger and Keith were still far behind. I looked out and down over the edge searching, praying for an answer. Before me lay a complicated labyrinth of tabletop mesas with layers of earthy red, orange, yellow, and purple. Each butte that made up the whole of the canyon was unique and had its own personality, shape, and style. The deep cuts in the soft rock told a story of tension and release throughout more millennia than I could imagine. I began to understand how the persistent unrelenting forces of wind and water had washed away each rock into its own unique shape. Now the rock was being what it was for a brief time, and by being true to itself, the beautiful infinite whole of one of the planet's most extraordinary landscapes was created—something imperfect and yet beyond human description of beauty. The words in my mind were inadequate; but I knew in that moment I had been changed at a cellular level.

Those rocks were like my life. Complicated, unique, my own style. Deep cuts of disappointment and emotional pain. Like the conundrum before me. Yet the rock didn't care that it had been washed away. Emotions came rushing in almost too fast to process: the shame of being foolish, broken, a failure, unworthy of another person's love. How had feelings of disappointment, deficiency, and fear shaped me? Why not be unique, broken me and create my own path? I took a deep breath, closed my eyes, and began to sob. My body shook as if I were in an impassioned mystical trance.

My legs could no longer hold me, and I collapsed down on the perilously narrow trail.

I don't know how long I lay there crying. Finally, I managed to pull myself to a sitting position and scoot over against the rock wall to drink some water. Dazed, I looked out across the Grand Canyon while I waited for my companions to catch up. I had experienced one other emotional breakdown during my senior year in college, but this time it was different—off the charts. It was as if every unresolved and hurtful relationship in my life had been pulled out of me and thrown into the abyss of the canyon. I was left empty—a good empty—and there was, for the first time I could remember, a feeling of safety all around me.

I heard my friends laughing as they drew near and hurried to wipe my face. Keith kept his distance pretending to take pictures, while Ginger approached. She sat down beside me and leaned against the red rock wall. I saw the concern in her eyes and told her as much of my story as I could understand then. She listened with a forgiving heart.

"I'm sorry I behaved like a bruised child," I said. "Having Keith around brought up a lot of emotional baggage I wasn't quite expecting."

"Yeah, I did notice," said Ginger and put her arm around my shoulder.

"Seeing you two happy together just made me feel how much I want a boyfriend. But you know better than anyone that brings up all my fears."

Ginger nodded and stroked my back. "Sounds like you've taken a giant leap in figuring things out, Helcat. I am so proud of you."

We sat quietly looking out across the canyon. Keith politely cleared his throat to announce his proximity. Ginger and I stood up and gave each other a long embrace.

"Everything's really okay, you know that," Ginger whispered in my ear. "And the best part of the hike is still ahead of us."

"Right Ginge. We're going to the bottom together—the three of us."

We continued on, and it wasn't long before I began to smile and even laugh. Water had transformed rocks into the deep wild beauty of the canyon, and the canyon had transformed me. It became my place of spiritual birth. Hardly a day goes by, even now, that I don't think or dream about it.

The hike out of the canyon on Bright Angel trail was effortless and fun. We women left Keith in the dust. The months of skiing, hiking, and bonding had made us truly strong. Perhaps it was because of my transformative experience, or maybe because it was Easter Sunday morning, but whatever the reason, Ginger and I sang as we climbed. Our lighthearted songs reflected new hope in that bright sun-filled day. We met hundreds of people who were brave enough to explore below the rim, including those who were part of the mule trains. From our perspective, the most dangerous part of that adventure was getting poked in the eye from the mule riders who were completely unaware of where they were holding their switches. It was tricky, as we hikers needed to be on the canyon side of the narrow trail to let the mules walk next to the wall for their safety.

Once at the Rim, we were excited to have a hearty meal of burgers, fries, and beer. Never in my life had food tasted so good. Conversation flowed easily, too. I didn't want the day to end but we all knew that our next stop was the Phoenix airport to drop off Keith. We found our car and drove along the South Rim, jumping out at each lookout to gaze one last amazed time before heading south.

The last step on our agenda before heading into L.A. was Joshua Tree National Monument. It was remarkable, but not in the way we expected. Yes, the scenery was unique and beautiful, the hiking trails well kept, the campgrounds uncrowded. Ginger and I both knew that our grand adventure of skiing the Rockies and hiking in the Southwest was about to end. We pitched our tent and prepared our favorite meal of tuna noodle casserole in silence. We knew each other's routine so well; we didn't need words. We moved in unison as we performed our camping chores. Once we were fed and our sleeping bags in place, we retreated to the car to get our journals. We'd made a regular practice of recording our adventures.

In the tent, I had no desire to write. Instead, I thumbed through the scribbled pages of the last few months, reliving what we had experienced.

"Do you remember the time we were in Bryce Canyon and those two handsome guys were walking ahead of us?" I asked.

Ginger looked up. "Right, and we accosted them with non-stop talking. We'd been alone together for so long; it was a major relief to have other people to tell our adventures to. They spilled out of us. When you would stop talking, I would pick up and not miss a beat." We giggled remembering the look of relief on their faces when we finally stopped talking.

I started laughing as I read a passage about a star-crossed cross-country skiing outing in Glacier National Park that seemed eons ago as we sat in the warm desert.

"What's so funny?" Ginger asked.

"Oh, it's partly me and partly the stupidity of the situation. Remember that time we went skiing in Glacier? We had Wendy from Australia with us. It was one of the few times we actually cross-country skied."

"Do I remember?" she said. "You were so incredibly frustrated with the skiing conditions. You kept falling down. The more you fell, the madder you got. I thought it was so hilarious, because it was usually me who was falling down on the slopes. It was fun to have the shoe on the other foot! I can just see your face as you fell for the umpteenth time. You yanked off your skis and said you were going to walk out of the woods, but the snow was thigh-high. That put you way over the edge. I had to bribe you with hot chocolate to keep going."

"Yeah, very droll." I was still smarting. "Okay, I'm embarrassed."

"Why did you get so angry? It was completely out of character."

"Well, I thought if I insisted we stop, you'd get angry with me. I was already tired when we set out on that trail. I had my period, and I was so exhausted I actually wondered if I'd ever make it out."

"Oh," she said. "I never realized you were afraid of me or tired. Sorry."

"Well, yeah. Back then I was scared that if you got angry with me, you wouldn't return from your side-trip to Seattle, and I'd be on my own. But now, I can laugh at

myself, because I know you well enough to voice my opinion. We've learned to work through whatever the issue is, haven't we?"

"Yep, we have. That's what friends do."

We both turned back to our journals. Joshua Tree was remarkable, because that was where Ginger and I sat in silence enjoying each other's company while we recorded our reflections on the whole magnificent journey that changed our lives. And we let ourselves wonder where the next journey would take us.

We took our time to break camp the following morning. It seemed both of us were putting off the inevitable; neither wanted to leave the lifestyle we had created for ourselves. Our route from Joshua Tree took us to Palm Springs, where we found a quaint lunch counter.

"You ready for this?" I asked, as we ordered a decadent lunch of burgers and salad.

"What? L.A.?"

"Yup."

Taking a deep breath and letting out a long sigh, Ginger said, "As ready as I'll ever be. I am ready to have an income again."

"Yeah, I'm looking forward to that part as well. I admire your guts in trying something completely different in an-oh-so-foreign land."

"I think we're both doing that," she said.

We sat in silence while we finished our lunch.

"You know," I said, "thirty, forty years from now, when I look back on this, no matter what great things I'm

doing or what I've accomplished, I'll still know this adventure was one of the best of my life. I've heard it said love is eternal, but I could only understand that theoretically until now. Sharing this grand adventure and getting to know you, now I understand. It's been like we're sisters. You've helped usher in a different me."

"Aw, I wouldn't go quite that far Helcat," she said wiping away a tear.

"No, I mean it. My life is on a completely different path than six months ago. I don't think there's ever enough repayment for something so big."

"No repayment necessary, Helcat. We've changed our lives together. And I do have a feeling that we haven't seen the last of each other."

Ginger (on right) and I getting ready to head into the Grand Canyon
©1990

·6·
Scorpion

I arrived back at Glen Canyon alone and a little scared—one of eight at the new ranger orientation. Dan informed us that another ranger had been hired, but wouldn't arrive for three weeks. There was only one other woman in the group. She and six rangers were to be stationed at mid-and upper-lake locations, so socializing with them over the summer would be non-existent. The incoming ranger would be stationed down-lake at the dam like me.

The first order of business was our housing assignments.

Since my housing over the past few months had consisted of youth hostels, motels, and a tent, I didn't give much thought to the ranger quarters. Surprisingly, my quarters turned out to be almost posh—a sizable room in a new, completely furnished, three-bedroom doublewide, perched at the edge of a marina overlooking the lake. Lakefront property at its finest on a ranger's salary—all this for only $90/month, utilities included. My housemate, Diana, a field biologist and native Arizonian, knew everything about nature in the desert. I plied her with questions. My second housemate was the other ranger, Lori, who would be arriving in a few weeks from Ohio.

While the 'up lake' rangers thought they had the keen assignments, being stationed at the busiest point of entry for the recreation area did have its advantages. Page, although not the most exciting Wild West town, had all of the modern

amenities, including what became one of our favorite retreats—the movie theater that let us sit in air-conditioned comfort to watch flicks and eat the gigantic dill pickles they sold alongside popcorn at the concession stand.

During the two-day orientation, I became keenly aware of how coveted National Park Ranger positions are, even if just for the summer season. Several new rangers were lamenting the length of time it had taken them to finally get called for a position.

"How long have you been applying?" I inquired.

"Two years…five years…six years," came their replies.

"Really?" I exclaimed.

"Well, how long did it take you?" they asked, frowning among themselves.

"Just once. Actually, both Kings Canyon and this park called me."

The room became extremely quiet. I had struck a nerve, with the men particularly. They looked at each other, then in an effort to console themselves, continued to bemoan the fact that they were called to work at a National Recreation Area, instead of one of the 'real' parks.

"Wow," I interjected finally to bring some levity to the grumblings. "I guess I hardly believe that people actually get paid to do such a fun job. *And* we get to wear these absolutely styling hats."

Determined to belabor the ill begotten fate, one quipped, "Well, at least we're not pseudo-Rangers like the ones at the Washington Monument in D.C.!"

In that moment, I knew I was thrilled to have 200 miles separating me from the complainers.

One evening, about a month later, I came home to the doublewide after a hot day of working the boat launch ramp. My housemates asked if I wanted to go to a movie. It wasn't hard to decide that an air-conditioned theater in town would be just the ticket.

Before heading out, I made a pit stop. As I stood up from the commode, I noticed something dark and not too small scuttling away near my feet. For a fraction of a second, I froze with fear and confusion, then let out a gasp. On the floor inches from my foot was the largest meanest looking scorpion known to humans! Well, at least known to me. My first-ever sighting! In hiking the desert so far, I'd never seen one, and it had not yet occurred to me that during daylight hours they lurked under rocks in cool dark places, like rattle snakes. I let loose a blood-curdling scream and raced from the bathroom pants still down not caring a bit about dignity. This creature was huge, and the world must be warned!

My two roommates immediately sprang into action. Diana, who was curious about why in the world I was screaming, put down her book and headed for the bathroom. I warned her to do so at her own peril. Lori, from Ohio, the organized one, equipped herself for the challenge with scorpion-catching gear: boots, long sleeves (it was 100 degrees outside), rubber kitchen gloves, a flashlight, tongs, and a glass container with top.

"You mean you're going to let this thing live?" I yelled at her.

"Quiet down. You'll scare it, and then you'll never find it," Diana said as Lori headed for the bathroom. Then she shook her head, unable to see what all the commotion was

about. "You Easterners," she said and sat down to go back to her book.

I followed Lori into the bathroom staying safely behind, thinking this way at least she'd get bitten first. I did my part and held the flashlight far out of the way.

"I don't see it, do you?" said Lori with trepidation. She scanned the small area, then pulled back the shower curtain. Nothing in the tub. Oh no, could this monster scale a tub?

"It was near the toilet over there," I offered.

Lori looked again behind the toilet, not getting too close. Nothing.

"I think the only place left to look is under the sink cabinet," she said bravely.

The beam of the flashlight shook as I tried to steady myself and back away. Lori took a quick peek and shut the door tight. Nothing in sight.

"How can that be?" I asked.

"They do crawl in from the vents," Diana called from the living room.

"Do you think it went back down the vent?" Lori asked her, not getting too close.

"I don't know. It's possible." Not much comfort from the other room.

"Let's put something over the vent and keep looking," I pleaded.

Lori found a book to place on the vent. Then she opened the cabinet doors again. I aimed the flashlight, and there, huddled in the corner, was the poisonous monster! The scary job became a race to catch it before it did us in. Lori bravely attacked from the side, pinning it against the corner,

then not quite securing it with the tongs. It struggled free. Her second attempt was better, but no go. I shrieked. It was headed toward us at lightning speed. Lori, the heroine, slammed the jar down on top of it.

Victory!

We raced into the living room with our prisoner in the jar, trying to screw on the lid with shaking hands. Lori displayed the monster scrabbling for freedom inside.

"That puny little thing?" Diana exclaimed unperturbed. "It's probably a baby. I've seen some three times that big."

"Oh, don't say that. Quick! Run outside!" I yelled in distress and pushed Lori toward the door.

She headed out with me at her heels, wanting to make absolutely sure she threw this thing as far away from our house as possible—like maybe into the lake. No such luck. Lori spared its life and set it free over a hill to join its brothers and sisters.

Later that night, flashlight in hand, adrenaline pumping, I stood on the bed and checked every crevice and corner of my room, under my pillow, every inch of my inside-out sleeping bag, and down my pajama legs. I was fully expecting to see a legion of the scorpion's angry relatives ready to seek revenge. Then I hesitantly settled in for an uneasy night, interrupted by scuttles in the corners and scritchings on my skin that caused panic. With the morning light, I had a new perspective on scorpions and their place in nature, and a new respect for our animal friends.

Being from the Northeast, I had never concerned myself with small crawly or slithery critters, but there were some rituals I rapidly developed. Rule Number One of the Desert: check shoes every morning in case a scorpion has

climbed in for a snooze, and check sleeping bag every night to make sure a slithery friend has not curled up there seeking warmth.

My hat and radio ©1990

·7·

Wearing the Hat

I loved working as a ranger. I woke exhilarated to begin my day, and every day seemed like a vacation to me. I didn't have to worry about scheduling enough staff for meals, fretting about rising food costs, keeping a restaurant clean or what to wear to look professional. People I dealt with were generally on vacation, in a good mood, wanting to experience our American Southwest, and somewhat in awe of the ranger uniform.

One of the best perks was living in one of the most awesome places on earth and demonstrating a way of living that would preserve and protect that priceless environment. I took the mission of preserving and protecting for future generations seriously and felt proud, honored, and humbled to play a small role in the immortality of that special place.

Most days, I worked in the visitor center. The overall feel of this busy port of entry was a bit peculiar. Thousands of people would converge out of nowhere, most believing Glen Canyon a brief stop on their way to somewhere more important. It was a great people-watching place. The characteristics of visitors ranged from laid back with all the time in the world, to stressed-out and intent on seeing this section of the world in four minutes or less. I liked interacting with the visitors who were hybrids of the two extremes. People with all the time in the world could be hard to get rid of, like gum stuck on the bottom of a shoe, while the stressed

visitor really just wanted to know the location of the nearest bathroom and how to get to their next destination.

The center, with its terrazzo floors, gigantic windows, and recessed lighting, coupled with the slight vibration of the enormous electric turbines located several hundred feet below, gave off a funky energy best described as a cross between sterile hospital and volcano about to erupt.

I was periodically expected to give talks about the area or on a subject relative to the area. In most ways, we were allowed complete autonomy in developing our programs. However, we were only allowed to give facts about the dam and urged to avoid engaging in debates over the environmental issues that the dam posed, such as altering the flow and banks of the Colorado River, the silt piling up behind the dam, or the evaporation of water from the lake in such an arid region. Initially, I was fine with that directive, although later I felt bound by it. I honed my interpretive skills by giving talks around the relief map. At times I felt like an automaton reciting the same things over and over. Usually I would take a visual poll to see if people were engaged. Facial expressions ranged from bored to content, with a rare look of intrigue. I tried upping the enthusiasm in my voice and breaking up my recitations with humor, a bit of trivia, or a side trip into a local newsworthy item.

When not at the visitor center, I was stationed at Wawheep Marina boat launch. On any given weekend, hundreds of boats were launched or came into port. My main duty was directing traffic to ensure that those coming off the lake and those wanting to go out on the lake didn't crash into one another. Safety and flow were the order of the day and

not always easily accomplished. Drivers of cars have different degrees of mastery. So do pilots of watercraft. The fun really began when the driver and the pilot possessed a completely different skill set. I think I should have received a degree in sociology for working on that boat ramp. Husbands, wives, and children completely transform their relationships based on who is in charge of the boat. The men tried to take over and be in charge; many of the women let them think they were in charge, although that was debatable. Smart children stayed out of the line of fire. I did see a few scratches and dents when whoever was in charge had missed the mark. Then the sparks would fly.

Campfire programs that I had been so worried about turned out to be one of my favorite functions. When I had a campfire, my schedule would shift to accommodate a later start to the workday. A typical campfire day would begin around the dinner hour, touring the campground to visit with campers and drum up business for the evening presentation. I was often invited to sit and share a meal. It always amazed me how generous people were to a female ranger in uniform, and that hat I loved was always a powerful symbol.

During one particular tour, the sunset was especially beautiful, even breathtakingly surreal. The way the sunrays lit up the crimson and orange rocks reverberated into the skyline and highlighted the blue water. I paused taking in the beauty. How I loved being outside at this time of day when being part of nature, not separate from it, seemed so natural. I realized how we have become good at separating ourselves from nature, people, and the world around us. We live in gated-communities to keep other people out, and we build bigger

houses to shield us from nature as a measure of success. And we kill animals to wear their hides so their hides can protect us from the weather.

I looked at the huge metal RVs parked so close to each other in the campground. They had every last comfort of home out here away from civilization—the American Dream of the open road. Yet actually these people were missing nature and the joys of being away from it all by staying inside a tin can parked ten feet from the next tin can.

While contemplating these insights, my moment with the amazing sunset was abruptly cut short by the unwelcome sound of the evening news blaring from a television inside the nearest RV.

Taking full advantage of my uniform, I knocked on the door and let myself in. A man dressed only in shorts didn't have time to get up from his chair.

"Sir," I said with authority, "how can you possibly be watching the news when you have the best seat in town for the world's most spectacular show?"

Shocked at this bold woman ranger standing before him and not knowing what to do, the man got up from his chair and turned off the television. He followed me outside, and we both watched the sunset in silent awe. I still wonder if he was too frightened and embarrassed to speak, or if he was moved by the experience. I'd like to think that maybe it transformed both of us into better, more appreciative human beings.

Another observation I had while perusing the campground was the different ways people roast a marshmallow. To some it was simply dessert after a cook out

or part of the activity of camping. To others it was an art form. After much observation and by popular demand, it was an art that I began to teach others.

This art form, I told the campers, was as much about the process and the person as it was about the end product. My own process would start by ever so gently pushing the marshmallow on the stick and taking care not to puncture all the way through. Let the pillow of sugar absorb the pressure. Stop just when you feel the point of the stick threatening to show itself.

Trial and error was required to find the perfect ember to roast over. I could see that people, particularly children, were tempted to shove the stick directly in the line of fire. To do so was detrimental to the art form. The perfect coals emitting gentle waves of heat lay deep beneath the burning logs. They beckoned, and the art of marshmallow roasting commenced.

Rotate the pillow of sugar slowly, I told them, so that the browning process can continue evenly on all areas, and be careful not to set the top of the marshmallow on fire and blacken it. Just when you think it's going to fall off the stick—it's perfect! The method was to slowly pluck it off by grabbing the very bottom. This ensured that the roaster would enjoy the entire delight.

One of the great things about the personalized piece of art they held in their hands, I told them, was that they could devour it any way they chose. Opinions differed on what was the best way to eat a roasted marshmallow. I watched many different techniques. Personally, I learned to leave the very top for last as it had the perfect combination of melted mallow and roasted crunch. No matter which method people chose,

there was nothing like dessert on a stick! It's interesting how simple pleasures like roasting marshmallows can even the field and bring people together.

As the season progressed, I experimented with different creative ways to involve people during my campfire programs. One of my favorites was the program on dinosaurs. I would measure out 70 feet and call up four people to stand in the appropriate spots where the dinosaur's legs would have been. This created an amazing visual of how massive these animals were.

One night, a dinosaur leg in my show was particularly handsome. As I was positioning him, I noticed that he had really nice biceps, too, and so I gently squeezed his arms and smiled at him. Not remembering that my microphone was on, I commented that the leg of this dino had really nice features, and I had definitely been alone in the desert too long.

Normally, a comment like that would have been heard by only a few in the front row. However, my microphone was on. I realized the statement was broadcast to one hundred people in the audience when laughter erupted from every corner of the amphitheater. Mortified, I did what any self-respecting sex-starved ranger would have done when a verbal filter fails—I exaggerated my embarrassment by stretching out my arms and giving him a hug. Lucky for me he was a good sport and hugged me back. I regained composure and continued with the program.

·8·

The Primary Rule of Desert Living

One day in July, I was given a special assignment at Lee's Ferry, located ten miles downstream from the dam. I hummed to myself as I drove south from Page toward Marble Canyon. The early morning desert vistas stretched out for miles. I smelled the dust and eternal dryness out the open window and thought I really am starting to feel at home here. Deep-cut canyon walls rose to over a thousand feet, making me feel insignificant, and the intense red and orange colors of the sandstone contrasted beautifully with a deep turquoise blue cloudless sky.

Lee's Ferry is the only spot within 200 miles south of the dam where sheer canyon walls do not hem in the powerful Colorado River. Its open valley allows access to experience the river. It actually was the site of a ferry crossing from the 1870s to almost 1930. Now people travel up river from there toward the dam for fantastic trout fishing, or drop into the Colorado for a wild and wonderful rafting trip southwest through the Grand Canyon.

My assignment that morning was to check the condition of the Spencer Trail, named for Charles Spencer, a late 1800s visionary who had plans to wash gold dust from the sloping banks of the Colorado. The trail is a series of switchbacks a couple of miles up the steep canyon wall to stunning vistas atop the Vermillion Cliffs. I had started out early, acting on the advice of fellow park rangers who'd told me summer temperatures there can reach triple digits by

midday. I found the trailhead around 8:00 a.m., checked my pack for water and food, and then eagerly started the climb.

The beginning was relatively easy, but the rapid rise in elevation soon proved challenging. The narrow trail follows along the steep sides of the hills, where broken red sandstone lay everywhere. By nine, the temperature had soared into the mid-80s, and I was hardly halfway up. I turned around, took a rest and drank water. The views were already spectacular! To the southwest, I could see the beginning of the deep Grand Canyon crevasse and the grays, purples, and whites of Marble Canyon. To the northeast, a rare full view of Lake Powell sparkled under the sun. The Colorado River far below wound through it all.

By 10 a.m., I was shocked to see that my two full water bottles were already approaching empty. I thought I had packed enough water that morning. Now I realized that unexpectedly hot temperatures had caused me to deplete my supply much faster than expected.

I squinted up toward the top of the red cliffs above me. The others had promised incredible vistas from the plateau on the summit. I had packed my camera and really wanted to bring home those magnificent views.

Buck up, I told myself, it's not so far. You'll make it. I walked on, but with every step became more aware of my quandary—I was extremely close to reaching my goal, *and* I was running out of water. Would the vistas be worth the risk of having my body found by a search and rescue team? I stumbled on for several minutes. Then I took time to breathe, gather my senses and check how I was feeling physically. The answer was unfortunately all too clear. I was light-headed, a bit dizzy, stumbling more, and becoming unsure on my feet.

Be smart, I told myself. Give up. I snapped a few pictures commemorating what I had achieved and reluctantly turned back down the trail.

As I descended, I tried to review what we had been taught about heat exhaustion. Was this what it felt like? I was more frightened step-by-uncertain-step. I stumbled over and over, but my legs seemed to have a memory of their own and kept moving down toward the life-giving Colorado. After a while it took real concentration to stay aware. I could feel my brain retreating into a dangerous white haze. I looked down at my watch. Noon. The sun was relentless in a cloudless sky. No shade in sight, nor others crazy enough to take this steep trail at the hottest time of day. Just make it to river, to the ranger station, I whispered to myself over and over. One more step, come on, just one more, now one more. Sit down, my body cried, take a rest. Look. You could lie down over there behind that rock and curl up. I upended the water bottles and shook them, swallowed the last few drops. My feet seemed very far away from my head.

I took deep rasping breaths and ordered myself to stay upright and move forward, but I began to stumble on even the smallest rocks. Finally, the river did seem to be getting closer. Then, all at once, the land flattened out and I found myself running to the edge of the river where I collapsed on the bank and put my head in the water to cool off.

Then I walked to the nearest potable water, drank as slowly as I could, and lay down in the shade of a large rock to gather my strength.

I tried to forgive myself for running out of water. How could I have known? Hey, you're an eastern girl, and climbing the Adirondacks is a whole different story. It's often about keeping ahead of the rain and leaping over stream after stream in the shade of tall trees. I climbed back into the car and sat for a while, staring off. Who was it that told me I could start out at six and survive? Next time pay attention to the advice, I told myself, and determined to be more serious about having more than enough water—the primary rule for surviving in the desert.

Once recovered, I headed south to Marble Canyon Lodge for food. That's where I met Anne. She was 82 years old, her long graying hair braided and hidden by an off-white fedora with a black ribbon. She wore earth-toned clothing and her skin was tanned and spotted with age. She told me she was a sole traveler in her RV.

"What brings you to Marble Canyon?" I asked after we ordered lunch.

"I've been travelling around the country and Canada for the last 25 years. When my youngest graduated high school, I sold my business and my house, bought an RV, and I've never stopped since."

I was intrigued by the boldness of this crone.

"Wow! You've been travelling almost as long as I've been alive," I joked. "What made you decide on a nomadic life?"

"Well, years ago my husband encouraged me to open up a lunch truck. It was his way of knowing that I would have an income. Shortly after that, he left, and we divorced. I raised six children on my own. When they were all out of the house, I decided the ticket was more fun and freedom."

"I say yea to that!" I interjected.

"Now I travel and when I get road-weary, I stay put for a while in my favorite places," she continued. "The RV

parks are wonderful. I have my mail sent to my son in San Francisco, so I know my monthly retirement money gets deposited.

"And of course, I visit my children. I might slow down one day, but not yet! My next trip is Alaska. I'm meeting a friend in Seattle next month, and we'll take the ferry up the Inside Passage. I've never been to Anchorage, so I am really excited."

"I've never been to Alaska either, but it's on my list for sure!"

Our food arrived, and as I ate, I contemplated what it would be like to live a permanently nomadic life. I remembered how happy I'd been that winter living out of my car and knew it would be something I'd enjoy—someday.

Lee's Ferry view from Spencer's Trail circa 1990

·9·

Donkey Dung and the Trail to Life

Rainbow Bridge National Monument is a popular mid-lake destination at the Recreation Area. I had seen enticing photos of the 290-foot-high sandstone arch at the foot of Navajo Mountain on the nearby Navajo Reservation. It was first on my list of don't-miss places to go on days off.

The natural rock formation was accessible in only two ways: a two-hour boat ride from Page with a short hike, or a two-day hike over the mountain via a trail within the Reservation. The beautiful ride up the lake just didn't seem quite adventurous enough. So, I gathered information from other rangers about the location and steepness of the Navajo Mountain trail, directions to it through the Reservation, and instructions on what water supplies would be needed.

I enrolled another adventurous being. Shannon agreed to come with me. She was a native of Page, a college student at Brigham Young University and a tour guide at the dam that summer. Two important elements of the plan were arranging our boat transportation back from Rainbow Bridge and getting my car back to Page from our starting point in the Reservation. Shannon's younger brother, Jason, decided that he wanted to join us, and he had a friend willing to travel with us to the trailhead and drive my car back.

From Page we headed east, talking excitedly about the coming adventure. We turned north into the Reservation and soon passed the Chapter House Community Center. The ten miles after that were deserted but paved; then we bumped

down onto a dusty washboard dirt road with sections of slick rock.

My initial thoughts upon viewing the Reservation from the road were of a sparsely populated, poverty-stricken place. There were weathered old trailers, their roofs and siding bleached by relentless sun and no phone lines or running water. The yards were dirt and sagebrush, each with at least three vehicles in stages of decay (war ponies if you will), as well as hungry-looking dogs of mixed breed and a variety of free-ranging animals from chickens to cattle.

On a closer look, most trailers also had a traditional Hogan set somewhere out behind. A Hogan is a beautiful round house constructed from natural materials, such as logs and mud daub. The door, positioned to welcome the rising sun, is often covered with a bright woven blanket. Unlike the sun-bleached metal trailers, these were structures which blended perfectly with the desert landscape. I learned later that the Hogan was each Navajo family's place of worship, retreat, and meditation.

Beyond the trailers, Hogans, and my own prejudices, the passing scenery was boldly beautiful. Sky and desert joined together in an endlessly interesting line. I was still training my eastern eyes, accustomed to rich shades of green, to appreciate the subtle hues of brown, tan, rust and gold, and how they intermingled to create a stark new kind of beauty.

Although the people on the Reservation seemed to take life s-l-o-w-l-y, the dogs were another story. About 25 miles into our road journey, a dog ran out of nowhere and started chasing the car! Soon his friends had joined him yipping and biting at the tires. Their behavior reminded me of street gangs pouncing on a victim. Since we had to travel slowly on the

bumptious, slick, unfamiliar road, the dogs were able to keep up for over a mile to the edge of their territory before they thankfully gave up the chase.

There were no street signs on the Reservation. We were having difficulty locating the trailhead. Finally, realized we were lost and decided to search for someone to ask. At that moment a trailer came into view and we pulled over to see four or five burly Navajo men sitting on derelict cars drinking beer.

"You go ask," my compatriots urged me.

I turned toward Jason with a pleading look. He shook his head.

"You live around here. You do it," I said to Shannon.

"No. You're older. You'd be better at it," she assured me.

Reluctantly, the appointed spokeswoman, minus her ranger uniform and feeling vulnerable, exited the car. The men ignored me at first and continued speaking to each other in Navajo. I waited for a lull in conversation, and then asked my question. Maybe they didn't understand English this far into the Reservation, and probably they had no idea where the trailhead was. It certainly didn't look like anyone there had done any hiking recently, as if any were crazy enough to take the long way over the mountain to Rainbow Bridge. They looked at each other with raised eyebrows. Finally, one spoke in English, followed by the others. They pointed in the Navajo way, not by using their fingers, but by a gesture of the head, pointing with their nose in a certain direction. They nodded here and there and sent me on down the road to another road on the left where they said the land grew mountainous.

After thanking them, I walked back across the dusty yard with all eyes following me. Suddenly I did not feel at all

sure about this adventure. On we drove, then turned left onto a rough road no better than a driveway. Bouncing up toward Navajo Mountain, we kept glancing around.

"Maybe that's the trail over there," Shannon said pointing hopefully.

Our driver shook his head. "I don't think so."

"Hey," Jason said, "see that clear space over there. That looks more like a trailhead."

"Wouldn't there be a sign or something?" the driver asked.

"Not on the Reservation," I said, trying to sound confident. "They seem to just know where things are."

We stopped at the most likely place and convinced ourselves it was right. Our driver looked worriedly from one to the other as we pulled backpacks and sleeping bags from the trunk and said goodbye. Then, shaking his head, he got into the car to drive back to Page.

As the car left a trail of dust, we three looked at each other, hefted our backpacks and set out for Navajo Mountain. Before us, the irregular hillside was littered with enormous boulders from a long-ago landslide. I tried to read the topographical map to determine where we were in relation to the dotted line of the trail, but that proved fruitless. By reason of deduction and landmarks, we thought climbing up the rocky ridge to the summit rather than walking around the mountain would eventually put us on the trail that clearly went over the top. We could see it on the map.

We set out up a steep elevation confident that we would get to the freshwater spring we'd been told about by nightfall. For the next five hours we climbed over and around gigantic boulders taller than we were in the midday heat of the summer sun. Finally, at the summit, exhausted and hungry with still no clear trail in sight, we admitted to each other that we were lost. A new game plan had to be made. The rangers at Rainbow Bridge were expecting us by 3 p.m. the following day, so our objective had to be getting there by then or to a phone.

But first, with daylight dwindling, we had to find a spot level enough to make camp. This was a challenge. There was not an abundance of perfect places. Finding a relatively level, non-rocky area turned out to be a challenge, but we eventually settled into a protected incline under a lonely stunted juniper tree.

After dining on the sandwiches we'd packed and unrolling our sleeping bags, I began to read a story to my worried companions out of the book, *All I Really Need to Know I Learned in Kindergarten.* I hoped it would take our minds off the worrisome matters at hand.

"Okay, so what are we going to do tomorrow morning?" asked Jason, interrupting me before the first page was done.

"Well, I guess we'll just have to go back down the way we came, then cut across the desert until we reach that main dirt road, and pray."

"I doubt there's a phone between here and the Community Center," Shannon said shaking her head, "and that was at least twenty miles back. We don't have near enough water for that."

"Maybe we'll be lucky and find someone to help us get back," I said hopefully.

"Yeah, if it's like the help we got on the way over, we're doomed," Jason said, his face grim.

"Hey, look up," I said to avoid desperation and craned my neck toward where the extraordinary desert light show of stars had begun. We all crawled into our sleeping bags, me still nervous about nocturnal creatures, and stared in awe at the sky until we fell asleep.

After a breakfast of a few handfuls of granola washed down with Gatorade-laced water, we packed up and began the long trek down. I wished we'd thought to leave some trail markings for us to retrace our steps since finding a safe way down proved exceedingly tricky. Time and again upon climbing down around one huge boulder, we would be stopped by a 30-foot cliff and could go no farther. With every back track, our faces grew grimmer. Progress was painfully slow. I was feeling guiltier by the minute for getting us into this challenging mess.

"I think I remember this rock," one of us would say hopefully, but the rocks all looked the same, and the sun climbed higher. I stared at the ground more and more worried as I walked, not wanting to face my companions. How could I have been such a fool and not prepared better? My ranger credentials were not helping me this time.

Then suddenly I stopped. There on the ground was something sprinkled among the sand and rocks. I bent down to touch it, smelled my hand, then turned and smiled.

"Hey, guys, come look at this," I called out.

The others came over and stared at the ground.

"Look at what?" They eyed me as if I'd lost my mind.

"Don't you see? It's donkey dung! We are home free!" That multi-purpose byproduct was about to serve a new innovative purpose.

"The sun's got to you," Shannon said, and rolled her eyes at Jason.

"No. Think about it. If we just follow the droppings and hoof prints, we'll make it down safely."

So off I went tracing along the faint trail, all of us searching for the next clue of donkey dung. We wound around rocks and skirted cliffs with little incident as we followed the animal's sure path, although we were left with minor scrapes, bruises, and not-so-baby-soft hands.

Down on the rough uninhabited road, we checked our water and found we had only a little left to cross miles of desert. We had started out with enough for one day, as we'd been told we could refill at the spring on top of Navajo Mountain. Once again, I had ignored the Western Primary Rule about having more than enough water! Off we went in the direction of the main road. Not a word was said as we trudged on.

We were on a forced march, driven by our desire to reach civilization alive. We searched for any sign of life—smoke from a Hogan, a faint sound of a car engine; anything would have raised our spirits. I stole glances at my companions and noticed the desperation on their faces. My mind raced between questions. Will we beat the clock so the rangers don't start calling in a panic? What if they did call? Would that finally clue others in that we were missing? What would happen when we ran out of water? How long would we have? I felt responsible for putting us in this dangerous situation. I had messed up again, just when I thought I was getting settled in to desert ways. We each finally drank the last drops of water as the sun hit high noon, and the temperature

continued to climb. We rested at every scrap of shade to avoid heat exhaustion.

After five arduous miles, we came upon an old Hogan without a trailer, set so far back from the road that I hadn't noticed it on the way in. Out front, an older man working on one of his five 'war ponies' was surprised to be interrupted by three thirsty, exhausted white kids in shorts with backpacks. He spoke very little English. We had made minor headway in our conversation, when a young girl of about sixteen came out of the house. She smiled and spoke to us in fluent English, graciously filled our water bottles from an outside well, and talked with her grandfather in Navajo about our need for a ride. As money is the universal language, we dug into our pockets, but only came up with an offering of eight dollars between us. It was twenty miles back to the Community Center, so we promised more money upon reaching civilization.

Grandfather nodded agreement.

Next came the choice of a 'war pony'. The old man chose a rusty Ford pickup that was seriously showing its age. He kicked at a flat tire. We three looked at each other. The girl assured us the truck was running and helped him change the tire. The one they put on had about as much tread as an egg! With the feeling of again taking our lives in our hands, we prayed for safe passage and loaded our gear and ourselves into the rusted-through bed of the truck. The girl drove us over miles of washboard roads. Bumping and banging around in the dusty back of the truck, I stared at the rolls of red dust following us and pondered a stark question. Would we have made it back if it hadn't been for donkey dung?

An hour later and with only ten minutes to spare until our three o'clock ranger deadline, we arrived at the Community Center, the location of the only phone within 50 miles. I called the rangers at the visitor center to relay a message to the rangers at Rainbow Bridge and tell them we would not be arriving that afternoon.

My travel companions reached their father, who agreed to come get us. Our Navajo companions waited with us under the sparse shade of the only tree. We were famished, restless, and very relieved. Several hours passed until our ride arrived. We paid our friends and were thrilled to be on the way back to our comfortable environment in Page. Once safely in the air-conditioned trailer, I plopped down in the comfortable living room chair and closed my eyes. A boring boat trip up the lake to Rainbow Bridge seemed just the ticket.

Rainbow Bridge National Monument
National Park Service photo

·10·

Slot Canyon Magic

One day in July, a woman walked up to me as I stood behind the counter at the visitor's center. "Can you tell me how to get to a slot canyon? I've heard they're somewhere around here."

It seemed like almost every day at least one person would confront me with that hopeful question, to which I did not have a clear answer, although I knew my job was to be, or at least seem to be, knowledgeable about various items of interest in the area. I'm a quick study and had done enough research to be able to satisfy the majority of inquiries, but the elusive slot canyons were still a mystery to me.

Slot canyons. What an unusual name. Kind of like "Head Smashed in Buffalo Jump". The title says it all, yet I was intrigued to find out exactly what "it" was.

When I asked my roommate Diana that night, I learned that a slot canyon is hard to find because it's hidden below the ground, kind of a cross between a cave and a canyon. It's significantly deeper than it is wide, and is formed by rushing storm waters cutting into the desert sand and wearing down the soft sandstone rock underneath. While at ground level these underground river canyon/caves may measure only three feet across in places, they can drop more than 100 feet down below ground to the floor. I had a hard time envisioning such deep slits and was intrigued why so many seemed so excited about exploring something so narrow and linear.

I also found out that slot canyons can be a deathtrap when local or distant rainfall causes flash flooding. With safety more than 50 feet above you at ground level, drowning in a flash flood is a very real possibility in a three-foot wide space.

So how do you find these mysterious formations was my next question. Putting on her native Arizonian hat, Diana began to explain the geological features of the desert that are consistent with canyons; how to research the probable areas where one could occur and plot out places to explore in Northern Arizona.

"Come on," I said, "I wouldn't have time for that and besides, I might fall in."

"Hmm, well, you could pay $30 to a Navajo native for a scenic tour—or ask the right people."

"Are you the right people?"

"I might be. But the ranger named Paul who's at the other station is a fanatic. He's lived in the area for years and knows the exact location of Antelope Canyon. It's the most extraordinary one around here. I mean really, Helen, get ready to have a transcendent experience."

Fortunately, it was dry the week before our adventure, and the sun was shining brightly when Paul and I set out. I had checked to see that no local storms were expected. We met at the Visitor Center. For safety, I went in to inform fellow rangers of our plans to hike Antelope Canyon. Paul offered to drive since he knew the area. He explained to me that there is an upper and a lower canyon, mainly accessible by ladders once inside, and he wanted to explore the entire length if time and energy permitted.

Much to my surprise, it was only a short 15-minute ride. The way people had talked, it had sounded exotic, as if it were halfway round the world. He had timed our start to reach some special places within the canyon and photograph them during the prime sunbeam hours of 10:30 to noon. The advantage during this time of day is that the sun would be overhead, bringing out the magical colors throughout the canyon.

He parked the car off the side of a dirt road, and we started out following a faint footpath through the dust and sage. It seemed like an average flat and rocky desert hike. I would have missed the non-descript disturbance in the earth that was the entrance without Paul's guidance. The crevice was just wide enough for an average adult to slide through. I hesitated. I was about to climb down into the earth, a foreign experience for an Adirondack girl, and with a man I'd barely met. He went first. Then I lowered myself into the unremarkable fissure and was surrounded by claustrophobic sand and rock. What was all this hype?

"I'm not so sure about this," I said as we crouched there. How would it feel being surrounded by rocks so far underground with no easy means of escape?

"Don't worry," Paul said, "I absolutely guarantee you won't ever forget this. Just be patient."

The descent was gradual at first. The trail that led underground was sandy with rocks strewn about and when I looked up, there was a small bright strip of sky shining through a dark slit in the earth above us. Soon the floor began to fall away, and we were faced with climbing down a perilous makeshift 50-foot ladder of logs and rope. At the bottom, we walked along a dry riverbed. I kept trying to see the sky, but

solid rock walls closed in on us and grew taller and taller over our heads.

"Is this it?" I asked disappointed.

"Just wait. Just you wait," he said leading the way.

Then it happened. With each step my anxiety lessened. Beyond the remarkable feeling of being held deep inside the earth with a slice of sky way above, we were suddenly in another world. The harsh desert colors became washed pastels here below. Soft shades of orange, red, yellow, purple and blue sandstone had been blended and sculpted into indescribably beautiful flowing configurations by the water that had washed through. Everywhere I looked there was an elegant grace in the patterns and shapes. The otherworldly columns of sunlight created a subtle changing magic that transformed everything. We walked deeper and deeper into the earth. Sunbeams changed from a blinding spotlight on the floor to playfully dancing over the walls of the canyon.

We were lucky enough to have the entire place to ourselves that day. Both of us felt silent reverence. We rarely spoke. When we did, it was in hushed tones. I would pause in open-mouthed awe around corners as moving light created ever-changing subtle hues along the gracefully sculpted walls. It was a spiritual wonderland. I again felt the unmistakable presence of the ancient ones. My wonder transcended into honoring the Creator.

At some points, the narrow passages only left room for one-way traffic. I waited for Paul to crouch and climb through, taking mental notes as to where he placed his feet and hands or ducked his head to avoid hitting a rock wall above.

He was an expert at maneuvering the narrow spaces. I mimicked him and not so expertly squeezed my way.

"You're almost through!" he said. "Keep going! Wait 'til you see what's waiting for you in here!"

The narrow passage emptied into an enormous room where a brilliant sunbeam illuminated one wall with perfect focused light. No matter where I looked, shadows made intriguing shapes. In the middle rose a stupendous formation in the shape of a large nose with sly smile. I imagined the smiling eyes. That huge face put me at ease, and I heard the spirit of the canyon, which said, "You are doing remarkably well. Your life is supposed to be fun. You're going to love what's in store for you, so, relax and smile more!"

We continued to explore the different parts of the canyon until the early afternoon. I was enjoying a gradual sloping walk occasionally ducking my head to avoid low overhangs or turning sideways to fit through, like threading a needle. We came to a 20-foot drop. Peering over the edge, I saw another homemade ladder held together by decaying rope.

"Down we go!" chirped Paul with a bit too much enthusiasm.

"You've got to be kidding."

"Well, it's either use this, jump or turn back," Paul said.

"How about you first," I said. "If the ladder breaks, I'll run for help."

He smiled and climbed down as I held on to the top. "Okay. Your turn."

With Paul holding the bottom, I climbed down trying to ignore the creaking and relieved to have crossed this second hurdle.

After turning around and round in the chamber below following the rays of light glancing higher up off the walls, we realized the sun was getting lower in the sky. The subtle quality of light in the slot canyon changed minute to minute, so it seemed the hike back was a completely different journey.

We crawled out of the narrow entry hole and hiked over the desert where the full glare of afternoon sunlight seemed an insult to our senses.

Slot Canyon © Helen S. Hossley 1990

·11·

Coyote Buttes

"If you think that was great, you should visit Coyote Buttes," Diana said when I related my adventure. "The Bureau of Land Management administers it. I know the ranger there, Skip, and I'll introduce you next time he's in town. He usually stops in at the visitor center. It's such a special wilderness area that visitation is limited. It gets harder every year to keep it a secret though."

As luck would have it, the next day Diana noticed a cream-colored BLM truck in the parking lot. Sure enough, Skip was at the Center. After she made introductions, she asked if he would take me to Coyote Buttes. Although polite, he hesitated.

"I do understand how special it is," I said. "I promise to keep the location secret."

Reassured, Skip agreed to take me.

The Coyote Buttes day finally arrived! Skip drove us in his BLM truck stating that he was going to make this an official site visit. He was the BLM ranger assigned to the management of the wilderness areas around the Paria Canyon. I was excited, knowing I was in for a treat. This time I double-checked my daypack for food, extra water, sunscreen, hat and camera film. With everything in order, we headed north into Utah.

"So, tell me, why is this place such a big secret?" I asked as we drove.

"You'll see. The rock formations are incredibly unique, as well as the land surrounding the area. Currently, there isn't any structure in place to control visitation. I'm the only BLM ranger for hundreds of miles, so policing it is a challenge," Skip explained.

"How long have you been a ranger?"

"Fifteen years. Most of them in this territory. We have a different management plan than the Park Service. We're about land use for all. Some people call us the Bureau of Livestock and Mines," he said with an ironic smile. "How long have you been with the Park Service?"

"Only since May. I thought this would be a fun job and so far, it has been—and much more."

The first of several stops on Skip's official site visit list was the Paria Canyon parking lot. The Canyon is a popular hiking spot. Some of the best slot canyon hiking, huge red rock amphitheaters and sandstone arches can be found there. We noticed a couple of cars at the entrance to a primitive trail. Remote camping was permitted and there were people breaking camp as we arrived. Five German hikers stopped us to inquire about the location of an area with unique rock formations. Skip, being the consummate professional, gave them instructions on how to get to a part of the Canyon that had similar formations. Before they could ask more questions, he got back into the truck and we continued on our tour.

"I know they wanted to go to Coyote Buttes," he said, "but until a management plan is worked out, it's best to keep the location as close to our vest as possible."

Within a half hour of our last stop along the Canyon, we were at the trailhead for Coyote Buttes. Parking the truck a short distance down the road, away from the trailhead, making a pit stop at the only outhouse within miles, we were ready. It was an official site visit, so Skip made note of trail degradation since his last visit as we walked.

"This was done by people on horses," he said, as he bent to examine hoof prints that made a pronounced trail. "It would take too many hikers to have this strong an impact in a short period of time. This trail did not exist the last time I was here. That's not a good sign. Once you locate the trailhead, it's way too easy to find your way to the rest of the site."

We did not know how fresh the tracks were, and continued on with the expectation of running into visitors. Skip led the way off trail to one of his favorite places—a 'trash' pile left by the Anasazi over 1,200 years ago. In the pile were discarded arrowheads and shards of red pottery. This dump was an unexpected treasure for me. My only study of the Anasazi had been in books, articles, a visit to Mesa Verde, and observing their ancient objects under glass in museums. It was exciting to sit next to the jumbled pile where I was able to pick up, turn over and feel curved shards of pottery and stone arrowheads, rub my thumb over them, and know that they had been left there by real people.

One arrowhead I picked up was clearly a practice one, an unfinished object. The right side was honed to a sharp point and beveled on one edge. I ran my finger over the bevel as I would a knife, and was surprised at how sharp the arrowhead still was—not enough to cut my finger, but enough to warrant caution. Its left side, held the rectangular shape of the stone from which it was being carved. The base of the

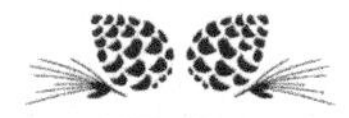

arrowhead had notches carved out which provided a smooth resting place for the rawhide to attach to the arrow.

I fingered a concave piece of pottery, the remnant of a larger pot or bowl that we estimated had been about five inches across. The interior of the shard showed marks of workmanship, and was black with stain as a testament to performing its cooking duties. The exterior displayed carving. I wondered how long this object had been in service before it finally succumbed to the stress of everyday desert living.

We followed the trail to the top of a ridge. My mouth dropped open at the magnificence. These striped rock formations hurled me into a new relationship with the Southwest. It was as if someone had taken multiple layers of orange, red, white, gold, tan, and brown putty, then stretched and pulled them in different directions, like taffy, to create long sloping smooth waves of color. Some formations looked like soft-serve ice cream cones while others were shaped in a large U with the different layers accentuated. In fact, one formation is called the Wave which looked like waves in the ocean.

In my wildest imagination I had never envisioned that rock could be so perfectly sculpted, malleable and intriguing. I could fantasize riding a skateboard up, down and over the smooth curved surface. I stood, unable to express the feeling of awe. I saw the remains of an ancient ocean that had worn away these gigantic waves and cones of sandstone.

Without a word, Skip led the way through the formations. We followed one rock wall, examining the gentle curves of its many stripes of color. I knelt down to run the palm of my hand over the abrasive texture of the sandstone, then stood up again, taking a step back and get a better look.

The stripes and curves ran beautifully symmetrical for several hundred feet. Then, as if someone thought no, that's not what I wanted, they took their galactic-sized hand, and smeared wet paint in all directions. The symmetrical lines became blurred, but once past this interruption, they continued on with their sharp edges as if nothing had happened.

"Maybe some giant creature threw a sand ball that went 'splat' and froze in time," Skip suggested.

I sighed. "These formations are alive," I told him. "I know rocks are inanimate, but there's something about the energy here. I'm having a very strong emotional reaction."

He smiled and nodded. "Yeah. It's kind of like the universe having primordial fun with its wild power. I've never met anyone who wasn't awe struck by this place."

Following on the glory of Angel's Landing in Zion, the funny looking sand castle Hoodoos in Bryce, the giant arches in Arches National Park, and my newly found spiritual connection with the Grand Canyon, Coyote Buttes was the culmination of my transformation. I could no longer pretend that southern Utah and northern Arizona were just another stop along the road to a better destination. I had always thought that my love of the Adirondacks, my home, could never be replaced. But now I knew it could be shared.

Coyote Buttes, The Wave © Helen S. Hossley 1990

Coyote Buttes © Helen S. Hossley 1990

·12·

Scratch, Scratch, Pause

When I was a kid, I was fascinated when we studied about petrified wood in school. I couldn't quite imagine rocks that used to be trees. Since then, I had wanted to visit a place called The Petrified Forrest. Now, this mystical fairytale place of my childhood was within driving distance.

I set out for a weekend adventure there, after making sure that my colleagues and roommates knew where I was going. With camping gear packed, I was ready to finally experience firsthand these rocky trees.

Petrified Forest National Park is about four hours southeast of Page, and I was excited to be on the road again. When I arrived, I stopped at the visitor center. The park is known for one of the largest collections of petrified wood in the world. Geologists from all over the world come to study its unique rock formations. Overall, I could see that the geography was relatively flat, with petrified log remnants of trees strewn throughout the landscape. These stone trees had been washed downstream thousands of years ago by an enormous flood, and became buried under sediment with a lack of oxygen. Mineral-laden water flowed down through the sediment and over the trees for many thousands of years. All the organic materials in the wood transitioned to stone. These stone logs were eventually deposited on open land.

The best way to explore The Petrified Forest was by foot. I parked my car at a trailhead, and set out in the direction of a popular site called Newspaper Rock. As many

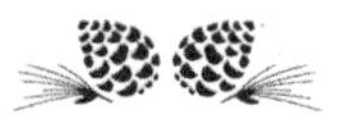

of the sandstone rocks in the southwest are exposed to wind and weather, the surface develops a thin layer of iron and manganese oxides, clay and organic material known as "Desert Varnish". When the varnish is scraped away, bright red rock appears. Newspaper Rock is no exception. In Navajo, the rock is called 'Tse Hone', which translates to 'rock that tells a story'. It has petroglyphs carved into all of its sides, many dating back 600 to 2,000 years. The ancient graffiti takes many forms: hunting scenes, kachinas, human faces, hand, bighorn sheep, antelopes, birds, snakes, and spirals.

While enjoying the feature, I noticed a man ahead of me pocket a little piece of petrified wood. I had to remember I did not have on my ranger hat, as I restrained myself from scolding. Yes, it was an awesome place, and a little souvenir would be a happy reminder. But it was also illegal. I had read numerous letters hanging in the visitor center of stories about the bad luck that had affected petty thieves. As a National Park Ranger, I had sworn an oath to preserve and protect the parks for the enjoyment of future generations. Our mantra to the public was, take only pictures, leave only footprints. With that in mind, I spent a glorious afternoon snapping pictures. I was fortunate enough to capture a close up of a handsome green and yellow collared lizard perched on top of a piece of petrified wood. I still have it framed on my wall.

The sun travelled lower in the afternoon sky. Since there are no campgrounds in the park, I had gotten a permit for backcountry camping in the Petrified Forest National Wilderness Area that shares a contiguous border with the National Park. This required a hike of one mile from the trailhead, to an area known as Litho Dendron Wash. I was

looking forward to the adventure of remote camping where everything had to be packed in and packed out.

A rough trail had been established in the dried-up riverbed called the Wash. To help me navigate, I used my rudimentary knowledge of reading the Geological Survey topographical maps, landmarks, and strategically placed rock cairns left by other campers.

Once I climbed out of the Wash, it was a steady upward hike to find any flat spot big enough to pitch a tent. I estimated I had walked about three miles before deciding to stop for the night. I set up my tent on a rocky mesa, arranged the sleeping bag and other gear, and sat there pleased with my cozy, and hard won, shelter. Although I was completely alone in a vast wilderness, the nylon tent brought a certain peace of mind, and sense of security, especially when it came to nocturnal visitors. I wasn't willing to sleep in the open with only a sleeping bag for protection. Snakes can't unzip zippers, but after my earlier scorpion run-in, I figured they could slither into a sleeping bag and cozy up undetected.

After enjoying the sunset with a PB&J sandwich, it was time to relax and watch the night sky's light show. I had underestimated the power of the complete darkness, as no artificial light intrudes on the night sky over the remote desert. The clear, dark, dome stretching over me allowed the pure brilliance of the universe to shine through. Even the tiniest faraway stars seemed bright that night. The Milky Way flowed over all like a light green river. Once I climbed into the tent, and opened the top window, I lost track of the number of shooting stars. It was a beautiful, serene way to fall asleep.

But I was having a hard time with sleep. My overactive imagination shifted into high gear. Am I really

alone out here miles away from everyone? There had been a few cars in the parking lot, although I hadn't seen anyone on the trails. Were they day hikers that took a different route? What if people had gone farther out than I was, and happened to make it back to this area? What about the four-legged critters? Some can be downright nasty when they are on the hunt for food. After all, I'm only another rung on the food chain. My heart began to race.

"Okay Helen, enough dramatics. Settle down. Take a deep breath." I said aloud in an effort to calm down.

"Count stars again," I instructed myself. I lay back in my sleeping bag, and began to count, as hundreds of fond memories of camping with Ginger filled my mind. I contemplated the amazing adventures I'd had with Paul and Skip over the past few weeks. Paul wasn't really my type, but I could see myself enjoying Skip's company. It was interesting that I could so easily entertain that thought.

I turned on my side and then it started. The sound! Was someone rubbing against the outside of my tent? I sat bolt upright. What if someone were hiking at night seeking out the only nearby landmark—the cairn sitting nearby that marked the trail leading deeper into park? That was ridiculous. Night hiking in the middle of the desert? I tried to calm myself and peered through the tent windows to assure myself that no one was out there. Only empty, moonlit desert in all directions. I settled back into my sleeping bag, heart still thumping.

I lay my head down on the makeshift sweatshirt pillow again, and started to drift. Then I heard scratching—again! This time I slowly rose from my position, trying not to frighten whatever it was. The scratching continued until I was

completely upright, then went away again. I unzipped the door, and bravely peeked outside the tent—nothing. Then, I turned on the flashlight to look all around inside the tent—just in case. Again, nothing. Hmmm. I sat, hugging my knees and thought, "that's odd". I settled in, and concluded, whatever was making that noise would eventually go away. If it had been a large predator, it would have certainly tried to attack by now.

In no time, the scratching started again. This time, I didn't move a muscle. I lay absolutely still, and listened hard. The sound was intermittent. And now that I really listened, it had a rhythm to it. Scratch, scratch, pause. Scratch, scratch, pause. I listened more intently. My mind raced to figure out what could possibly be so faint, yet so pronounced. It had timing, a rhythm. Could it be a snake? No, they are silent. A rodent? Maybe, but their scratching was faster and more irregular. An insect? Why didn't I hear a buzz instead of a scratch? I closed my eyes to focus my mind. Scratch. Pause.

Wait a minute!

I opened my eyes. Scratch. Pause.

I blinked. Scratch, scratch, pause.

Then I laughed to myself. It was my eyelashes rubbing against my sleeping bag!

"Helcat, you nincompoop," I could hear Ginger say with a smile in her voice as she turned over to sleep. She had always been the best antidote to my fears. I laughed at myself. The fearless lone ranger rides again.

·13·

On the Rim

I cherished my days off. They allowed me time for solitude after a week of greeting, and talking with thousands of people. It was my special time to hike into the desert where, I could listen to, observe, and commune with nature. I was also learning to be by myself, and enjoy my own company.

As fall approached, my time in the southwest drawing to a close, I decided to make a trip to the North Rim of the Grand Canyon, which was only a couple of hours drive from Page. The coolness of the air due to higher altitude, and oncoming fall, was a welcome relief from the desert heat. My plan was to arrive at the North Rim early enough to get a backcountry camping permit. While in the backcountry office, I did a bit of research to familiarize myself with the North Rim trails, hot spots, and points of interest; deciding that the flat Widforss Trail was the best option for overnight camping.

I had time to hike near the lodge before heading out, spending most of my day on the Bright Angel Point, and the Cape Royal Trails. I took in the glory of the canyon from a different perspective, and marveled at the beauty of the world's most majestic vistas that were constantly changing colors throughout the day. When the sun got lower in the sky, I knew it was time to begin the five-mile hike along the Widforss, set up the tent, then sit back to watch a glorious sunset settle behind the South Rim.

As my experience at the Petrified Forest had proved, staying in the backcountry, even for one night, exposes you to a vulnerability you don't usually experience in the comfort of civilization. You prepare, plan, and carry in all that you need to survive—food, water, shelter, and clothing—but planning, as I had learned, requires careful forethought and imaginative anticipation. Hiking and surviving in the backcountry was a way of life, and a particular mindset, I was still developing.

I left my car in the appropriate parking lot, and rechecked my pack to make sure I had everything I needed for the overnight experience. Tent, water, food, clothing, sleeping bag, flash light, permit. Satisfied, I set off.

The trail was relatively flat, well maintained, and not heavily traveled. I decided to run in order to make up the time I had taken earlier in the day, and see the sunset. While at a full jog, I came up over a small hill, and in the clearing stood a mule deer. We both were startled, and froze in our tracks. Once it registered that I was not a threat, it walked away, and we both continued on our journeys. After running for about a mile, I estimated that I would have just enough daylight to find an ideal spot to pitch the tent, and settle in next to the edge to experience the sunset.

While I was setting up, I was thinking about how nice it would be to open a cold beer to go with my chicken and rice dinner. Water, somehow, didn't seem quite festive enough for this last adventure. But water was the default beverage. After my tent was secured, I grabbed the container of dinner, and headed out to find the best view from the rim.

It was then I heard a helicopter in the distance, and thought it might be a sunset tour. Soon, I saw it was the

National Park Service completing its daily fly-by to ensure no unauthorized people were staying in the backcountry. It whirled by me, heading east, then abruptly turned around, and hovered above my head. The noise was deafening and the tornado from the blades, intense.

Above the noise came a booming voice, but the copter muffled what was being said. At first, it sounded something like, "m m m m m ear." Puzzled, I looked up at them shielding my eyes and straining again, to hear. They repeated what sounded like, "Do you want a beer?" Incredible! How did they know I was thirsting for beer? Perhaps this was the best curb service in the world delivering my exact wishes? Then I thought, wait a minute. It isn't illegal to have beer in a National Park. Why are they looking at me so insistently? Finally, it clicked! They were more likely saying, "You are NOT supposed to be here!"

In exclamation of understanding, I raised my hand with my index finger pointed to the sky, and ran back to my pack to shuffle through, and retrieve my permit. I ran back to the edge where the waiting helicopter was still kicking up dust. Thrusting the permit above my head with both hands, I smiled up at them. They waved good-bye, and flew off into the sunset.

Normally, knowing that the Rangers were out patrolling the territory would have brought a sense of relief. This experience made me wonder how many other people were on the north rim that night.

Suddenly, it seemed there might be something unnerving, and vulnerable about a woman being there all alone. Although I was in the backcountry, perhaps I'd chosen

a trail that was too easily accessible. The park patrol had highlighted the fact that others could be around. Over the summer, I had spent nights camping by myself, but most of the sites were walk-in-a-mile-middle-of-nowhere, such as in the Petrified Forest, or in a proper campground with other people close by.

This is ridiculous, I thought, as I knelt there before my tent missing the glorious sunset. Stop worrying, will you? You're a ranger remember. You simply cannot give in to this fear. The idea of striking camp and hiking five miles to my car over unfamiliar terrain in the dark was particularly unappealing. I decided to stay put, and settle in whatever the night might bring. Once in the tent, I thought how funny it was that a thin piece of nylon could bring me a sense of security.

My thoughts raced back to another unnerving camping experience. Ginger and I were setting out to hike along the Rio Grande River near Taos, New Mexico. A forest ranger met us at the trailhead.

"I want to warn you that a mountain lion has been sighted in the area," he said. "You two should be aware and be cautious."

We looked at each other, then back at him.

"Well sir, what exactly does cautious and aware mean around a mountain lion," Ginger asked.

"Well, if you do encounter one," he said, "make yourself appear as large as possible, and make noise so you won't be confused as prey. Make eye contact with the animal. Aggressively wave your arms, and act like a predator. Then slowly create distance, and if necessary, fight back using

anything you can to protect your neck and face. You'll be fine, I'm sure. This was yesterday, and the animal is probably miles from here by now."

We bravely continued on our planned hike, and tried not to think of potential dangers on the trail. It wasn't until the wee hours of the morning that I was awakened by a noise outside our tent. Not wanting to alarm Ginger, I pretended to be asleep, all the while listening intently to the disturbance, and scratching a few feet away. Eventually the noise subsided, and I drifted back to sleep.

When we woke in the morning, I asked Ginger if she had heard any noise. She confirmed that she did, and she, too, didn't want to alarm me. Then she added with a laugh, "All I could think of, Hel, was that you were closer to the door. I hoped whatever it was, would eat you first!"

"Gee, you are one heck of a friend. Thanks a ton!"

With that uneasy memory playing in my mind, thoughts shifted back to the North Rim. Why did I feel so alone, and in danger here? Maybe because human predators were worse than animal ones? I tried to talk myself through, and out the other end of my fear. What was really the potential of something more dangerous than a mountain lion lurking out there in the dark? Whether real or imagined, my fear was paralyzing. I lay there stiff, and unsleeping.

The skylight of my tent framed the stars and treetops perfectly. I thought a little stargazing might calm an overactive imagination. I turned off the flashlight and let my eyes adjust to the darkness. Slowly, the universe of twinkling stars came into focus. You simply don't realize how many

stars there are until you've been out west and camped out under a truly dark sky.

Try as I might, I couldn't shake the feeling that I wasn't alone. Every little sound was amplified in my mind—a snap of a branch, the rustle of the wind, the sound my body made against the sleeping bag as I shifted into a more comfortable position. I consciously slowed my breathing, and tried to center. All I wanted was to become invisible in case someone or something was creeping around out there.

Long slow breaths seemed to have more of a calming effect than stargazing. After half an hour, I did feel calmer. Calm enough to let my mind entertain other more productive thoughts. Thoughts like everything is really okay; it will be daylight before I know it; it's just a little wind stirring the trees out there and billowing the sides of the tent. Slowly my mind relaxed. Long deep breaths, eyes fixed on the framed outline of the stars. I could feel my muscles release.

This is more like it, I thought, a better use of my wild imagination. I began to even enjoy the experience. Before I knew it, I opened my eyes to find that the sun was peeking over the northeast rim. I was still, very much, alive! A feeling of gratitude flooded over me. I was grateful for my own soothing powers that had allowed me an experience never to be forgotten. That event was a milestone as I knew I had walked to the edge of fear, given it a handshake, and brought myself back to a great life.

Enjoying the North Rim before setting out on Widfross Trail
circa 1990

Bright Angel Trail looking into Indian Gardens

·14·

Now What?

It was mid-September, and there was a noticeable change in the weather. Rain and cool breezes replaced the oppressive heat of August. The evening temperatures were comfortable enough that we could turn off our evaporative swamp cooler. I had gotten used to its constant hum, but discovered once again, the quiet sounds of nighttime.

With everything winding down, crowds began to thin; there was a lack of lines at the marina boat launch, and sparse attendance at campfire programs. It was like the air was slowly being let out of a balloon. What a welcome change for the ranger staff. We finally had time to breathe, and enjoy our favorite places without crowds.

I was tempted to tackle a trip to Rainbow Bridge again, but had a better offer to take a prop plane supply ride up lake to Bullfrog, the farthest north marina. By car, it would have been a lengthy 400-mile round trip. By plane, it took a little more than an hour.

The day of our trip was overcast, and rainy. The only passengers were the pilot and me. I had never had a front row seat in a small plane before. Flying in a two-seater is sensual, as you can cruise close to the ground, following the contours of the landscape. From this new perspective, the scenery below was spectacular. Rain gave deep rich color to the red, orange, and purple rocks of the Vermillion Cliffs. Flying above the wide, cerulean lake contained by red rock canyons,

and accented by mesas, was like seeing the relief map at the visitor center come alive.

The pilot dropped down to fly a few hundred feet above the canyon walls. While at that elevation, we were unexpectedly buzzed by two noisy fast-moving jets. My heart was in my throat.

"Whew. That was close," said the pilot.

"Yeah," was all that I could get out.

"I wonder if there are more of those guys." He climbed to a safer altitude, then radioed headquarters to see if the jets had authorization to fly within the canyon walls. The report said that it was a film crew filming a spot for an upcoming special on Cher.

The rest of the ride was, thankfully, uneventful. We arrived at Bullfrog with a story to tell as we unloaded supplies.

As October drew near, my seasonal assignment was coming to a close. I had been having so much fun, learning, adventuring, and growing into myself, I hadn't really thought about what came next. The other rangers seemed to be chasing after the coveted full-time status, and already had their winter assignments. I wasn't sure if park jumping was something I wanted to do. The locations of the winter positions seemed to be in places that didn't appeal to me—like Florida or Texas.

"Diana, this is your second year with the Park Service, right?" I asked my roommate one night.

Curled in the living room chair, she looked up from the biology books she was always reading, "Yeah, it is. Why?"

"This seasonal work thing is new territory for me. I don't know what to do."

"Well, last year it was easy for me. I was still in college, so I knew I didn't need a winter assignment. This year I'm going to go back to Prescott for a while to visit my parents. Then I'll be taking a job on a fishing boat as a research biologist."

"I know most of the other rangers already have their assignments. I feel like I just don't know what questions to ask."

"Are you wanting to stay with being a ranger?"

"I'm not sure yet if I want to make this into a career."

Well, just talk to the others. See what they say. I mean, opportunities do seem to fall in your lap with some regularity, don't they? You'll know what to do."

I still wasn't sure what I was looking for, and felt more lost by the day. My seasonal assignment ended by default. I decided to visit Ginger in L.A. while I figured out what my next move could possibly be.

Everything seemed uncharted, and scary. I packed my car, and stood back to take one last look around. I scanned the comfy house remembering fondly my first encounter with a scorpion. One last time, I drank in the beauty of the lake, and recalled the cool rejuvenation of my nightly ritual swim after work. There were clouds around Navajo Mountain. I marveled over the beauty of the red, and orange canyon walls. Still rotating, I saw the marina come into view, full of houseboats docked for the season, and void of the life they held, seemingly only moments ago.

On my car, the skis were waiting for another season. I thought they looked lonely without Ginger's skis next to them. I hugged Diana, and our neighbors, then climbed into my car, backed out of the driveway, drove out of Glen Canyon National Recreation Area, and onto Highway 89.

I followed the path Ginger and I had driven when I dropped her off in the spring. It was strange not having any home base to return to. I hated to leave the canyon country that had captured my heart and soul. My destination was only an 8-hour drive away. I extended my adventure to visit a few more places on my list—Yosemite and Death Valley. I decided to treat myself to a coastline drive as I made my way to Monterey to pick up Route 1. I stopped for the night in Big Sur, where I slept in my car.

The next day, it wasn't easy for me being reintroduced to the jungles of California civilization. I arrived at Ginger's apartment in L.A., and was greeted with a long hug. It was as if we hadn't seen each other in years.

"Wow, I am so happy to be here with you." I said as we unloaded my car.

"Welcome to L.A. Helcat," she said as we walked through the hibiscus-lined courtyard to her one-story studio apartment.

It didn't take us long to dig into the details of each other's lives. Ginger's consisted mostly of working for an employment agency, and exploring the area on her days off, which seemed none too plentiful. I felt a little guilty as I had the best job in a playground beyond imagination! Keith had just completed a visit, and returned to the East Coast. My arrival timing was perfect as Ginger needed a pick-me-up.

"So, any wedding plans yet?" I asked.

"We've been talking about it. I do want to marry him, but I like my job and living in L.A. A long-distance marriage isn't in the cards. So, we'll wait. What about you? Any prospects in Arizona?"

Ginger went to the fridge, pulled out a couple of beers, opened them and handed one to me.

"Nope—and that's okay. I let myself go on a couple of dates. That was a big step for me. But nothing serious. I did have an amazing summer. I grew—a lot."

"That's good to hear on both counts. Now what?"

"'Now what' is the big question, isn't it? I'm hoping you can help me figure it out."

"Well, it's good to know some things never change!" Ginger laughed. "Here's to figuring it all out!"

We clinked our bottles together and drank.

We spent the next day's enjoying each other's company again, and sight-seeing as much as our meager budgets, and Ginger's time, would allow. For two weeks, while she was at work, I had time to reflect. The more I drove around, the more I discovered that I did not like L.A. one bit. Yes, the weather was beautiful, but there was something artificial about it. I could not picture myself living there. Washington, D.C. popped into my mind. I couldn't explain why there would be a pull to go back east at that point, but I had to admit there was.

"Ginge," I said one night over dinner.

"What's up Helcat?"

"I've decided L.A. isn't for me. As much as I would love to live out here near you, I think I need to go back east. I

don't know why, but I feel it's where I need to be. I'll miss you so utterly," I said with tears in my eyes.

"Oh, I'll miss you too, Helcat. But you need to trust your intuition. It is always right."

"I think I'd like to get going within the next couple of days, so I don't hit too much snow in the Rockies. I'll stop in Colorado Springs and then beeline it to D.C."

"Sounds like a plan."

We spent the rest of the evening deep in conversation about all the questions in our lives. Too soon, Ginger helped me pack my car, again, and we held each other tight as we said our good-byes. I climbed into my car. I drove down her street and watched her watching me drive away in my rear-view mirror. Then I cried until I reached the Nevada border.

A month later, I was living in an ugly rented room in an unsavory part of D.C.

"Oh Ginge, my life is in the TOILET!" I wailed over the phone, choking back tears.

"What's up? I thought you wanted to be in D.C."

"I did. But now I have no social life, and no job, and absolutely nothing is working out."

For twenty minutes she listened as I complained. Yet, even though it wasn't looking good, I couldn't shake the conviction that this was the place I was meant to be. As only a best friend could, she offered counsel. "Well look. Why couldn't you check out a Ranger position there? All those parks and tourists. There must be something."

Now why hadn't I thought of that? I started to smile for the first time in a week.

The next day I called the main office for the National Mall and inquired about their ranger needs.

Image courtesy of the National Park Service

·15·

The Washington Mall

"Hi. I was wondering if you're taking applications for ranger openings?"

There was silence on the other end of the phone at the main office for the National Mall.

"Hello?" I said.

"Uh, well, yeah," said a man's voice. "Sorry. It's just that we don't get many calls about ranger openings here."

"Oh, why not?"

"Well, with so many other government jobs around, being a ranger is usually last on everyone's list."

"Well," I said with renewed confidence, "I was a seasonal ranger out west last summer, and thought it might be fun to do that here."

I found out there was always a need for experienced rangers on the National Mall. Not many were clamoring to ranger in the city, and if so, they were short-term, impatient, and on their way to a coveted full-time National Park Ranger position somewhere more exciting, and wild. People simply don't consider the National Mall a park. It has memorial buildings, statues of famous people—and a glut of politicians. What's the fun in interpreting a building or statue or, heaven forbid, talking politics? Not much nature in sight except for a few cherry trees, a Canadian goose or two, paddling on the

shallow cement reflecting pool, and acres of grass. Nonetheless, I applied for a position and prayed it would work out as the little bit of money I had, dribbled away. Within a month I was hired.

Moving out of the ugly apartment, I found a tiny affordable apartment in Columbia, Maryland. It was about an hour commute, and I vowed to search out something closer within the year. I began work on the Mall on March 1st, choosing the evening shift. Working nights gave me time to explore the different venues on the Mall before my shift started at 4 p.m. I climbed the stairs, and stared up at the imposing marble statues of Lincoln and Jefferson gazing down from their august memorials. I zoomed in the elevator to the top of the Washington Monument to admire the view out over the reflecting pool to the west, our majestic Capitol to the east, the White House to the north, and the Jefferson Memorial to the south. I gazed at people weeping as they reached out to touch the names of loved ones on the Vietnam Veteran's Memorial Wall. The Mall at night had a special magical beauty.

It occurred to me that this job would be deeper, and more complicated, than memorizing the names of lizards, cacti, leading campfire programs, and marshmallow roasts. Could I really take on the daunting task of accurately representing the variety of details of our nation's history, art, and architecture? My interpretive skills would need serious sharpening with such a large variety of topics in which to be proficient.

Using the luxury of slow wintertime visitation, I studied hard, researched, memorized, observed—and reserved judgment, about serving at this park. I remembered the scorn

of my colleagues out west who said that working at the Washington Monument was a fate no ranger should have to endure. That spring, I came to appreciate the unique duties, challenges, and privileges facing me.

Working on the National Mall turned out to be an exciting experience. I developed my interpretive skills to a higher level. There were a large variety of topics in which I had to become skilled. I enjoyed the sites at which I served. There was never time to get bored in the rotation. Twenty million people visit the Mall every year from hundreds of countries, around the world. Each visitor has his or her unique viewpoint, curiosity, and questions about the United States, and its capital. There were constant challenges to answer these questions, and to accurately represent our country's history.

·16·

The Chip on Lincoln's Shoulder

The Lincoln Memorial was built in 1914 to look like a grand, Greek temple. It stands ten stories tall, with thirty-six Doric columns and friezes, inscribed with the names of the states. Some thought it far too ostentatious for a man of Lincoln's humble character. A simple log cabin shrine was proposed, but not accepted.

I always stopped to catch my breath as I walked up the mountain of steps to reach the gigantic chamber. I would turn around before entering the chamber, to take in the reflection of the dome of the Capitol building in the pool. What a relief to think that Lincoln was still keeping an eye on Congress.

I remember my first time entering the chamber. Tennessee pink marble floors contrasted with the stark white statue. Lincoln's statue is one of the most exquisite in D.C., due to the talents of the sculptor, Daniel Chester French, who, worked from a life mask of the face and hands. I was drawn by the intensity of Lincoln's stare. There were times when I thought he would rise up out of his chair, clear his throat, and give a lecture. Other times, when school groups were being unusually disrespectful, I wished that he would!

I had never been in a building with such acoustic resonance. Whisper in one corner, and it would be heard in the opposite corner. This was a good thing, except when 200 visiting school children were caterwauling. The noise was so deafening I could not hear myself talk. Luckily, I was most

often assigned to work the evening shift when the crowds were a bit more subdued.

One night, I noticed that we had more than ample staffing at the Memorial. I approached Nelson, a veteran D.C. ranger.

"What would it take for you to show me the attic?" I asked in a low voice. I had heard other rangers recanting wild stories of being up there, and looking down into the lap of the statue.

"Oh, you could probably twist my arm," he replied with a grin.

"You've been up there?"

"Yep, several times. I warn you, it's tricky. You have to watch your step. One misstep, and you could fall through the ceiling onto the Tennessee marble floor down here. A mess to clean up, not to mention the paperwork."

I laughed. "Sounds challenging."

"Well, are you up for adventure, a tight rope walk, and some nice views."

"Yep. Do we need authorization?"

He looked around, and smiled. "Right. Now, just who do you think would give us authorization?"

I shrugged, and rolled my eyes.

"Well, it looks like Jim has the floor covered," he said. "I guess I could go now. Get a flashlight."

On the northwest and southwest walls were iron doors that led to break rooms, and staff bathrooms. We slipped through one, continued though another door that opened onto a dusty steep stairway that led to the attic. In the dim light, Nelson turned on his flashlight. Within seconds, we were

standing at the threshold of the enormous, echoing, pitch-black cavity above the ceiling. I shined my flashlight up into the twenty-foot clearance between the Memorial ceiling and the highest part of the roof.

"Okay now. Really watch your step," Nelson cautioned, flashing his light along what should have been the floor. But there was no real floor. There were only ceiling tiles, made out of Alabama white marble that measured three feet by six feet.

"Those babies weigh about 75 pounds each," he warned me, "and they need to stay where they are unless we want to pick off a tourist or two. We have to walk between the ceiling tiles on the metal supports that hold them." He pointed at the metal supports that were only about six inches wide.

I grimaced, and stayed where I was. "Uh—that looks a whole lot easier said than done."

He showed me how to carefully place one foot in front of the other on the metal supports that held the tiles, and balance with arms out. "Come on. Let go. Be an acrobat, Helen," he urged, and smiled at the challenge. "You trod in the footsteps of many a ranger before."

I couldn't let myself be a coward, so I held my flashlight in my mouth. It was like walking on a tight rope between a giant checkerboard. Balancing precariously, I followed him to the ceiling grates, and spotlights positioned above Lincoln's head to illuminate the statue at night. There we could sit, and peer down—way down. My head started to spin! My heart rate jumped at the idea of being up so high without, what seemed like, real support. From this perspective above the tilt of Lincoln's head, I could see the curls, and part

in his tousled hair, the enormous size of his feet, and the artistry of how his arms and hands were placed on the arms of the chair.

"Some people say the sculptor arranged his fingers into the sign language for his name, but it's not true." Nelson told me, noting some of the curious detail's we rangers learn.

"Hmm. So, this is what the pigeons see when they land on Lincoln's head, huh?"

"Damn birds! What a cleaning bill," Nelson said. "Hey. Let's see if we can get up to the second frieze to look out toward Arlington Cemetery. It's a super, amazing view."

It was tricky approaching the second frieze of state names that ran around the top of the building. Beyond the grates and spotlights, a six-foot length of one ceiling tile stood between a vertical iron ladder set on the sidewall, and us. That tile happened to be the one placed directly behind Lincoln's head. A two-by-six board sat delicately atop this tile to displace the weight of a person as they lean to reach out, and grab onto the iron ladder against the wall that allowed access to the roof.

I began to panic. What if I missed the board, and stepped too hard on the tile? What if I made it to the roof, and couldn't get back down? How would we explain ourselves after a cat-in-the-tree rescue? We'd been gone awhile already. What if the other rangers ratted on us?

He was already halfway up the ladder.

"Nelson, stop!" I called out. "I-I think I've seen enough. Let's head back down." I was trying to sound calm as I chickened out.

He looked disappointed. "Oh, come on. Are you sure?"

"Yeah. Why don't we come back another time?"

"All right, easy does it now."

We retraced our steps, and made it back to the east side of the Memorial where he stopped to open the door that led out to the lower frieze. As I climbed out into the night air, before me lay, what I had hoped to see when we embarked on this adventure; a picture perfect view of the Washington Monument accented the reflecting pool, and the Capitol, both lit up in all their golden nighttime glory—and, best of all, no obstructions from visitors clamoring to get the perfect shot. Ironically, I did not have my camera with me, and made a mental note to carry it at all times in case other acrobatic photo opportunities presented themselves. But that night, I settled for an indelible mental image that I remember to this day.

We finally turned our backs on the grandeur, and made our way downstairs to the din of excited colleagues. Our secret was out.

"Well, did you get to the top?" my fellow ranger, Christopher asked, his eyes alight.

"No, only to the first frieze, but I did peek down into Lincoln's lap," I reported.

"Totally cool," he said. I could tell he wanted to follow in our footsteps.

Christopher was a history major at Brown University. The seasonal ranger job on the Mall seemed like a great fit for someone studying history. He had settled well into his ranger duties. It was spring, and nice to have additional staffing for the kickoff of the summer season.

On Memorial Day weekend, at 11 p.m., a call came over the park radio that a patient from a nearby mental hospital had escaped, and was presumed dangerous. The last known sighting was around the nearby, Vietnam Veteran's Memorial. Those of us working at the Lincoln Memorial went into high alert.

I stared at the ceiling. Prior to the call, Christopher had decided to take five of his visiting college friends up to the attic, and the second frieze. It was a terrible, risky idea, and other Rangers had tried to dissuade him, but he was determined. While up there, he was unaware of the tension happening down below, as he did not have a radio with him. On the ground it was all hands-on deck. No one could run up into the attic to warn Christopher and his friends. Yelling up to him was pointless.

With each passing minute, we became more anxious. Our only defense was a telephone with the hope of having the nearest police respond immediately. Upon reflection, the emergency training of interpretative rangers was woefully inadequate even though we were usually the first line of defense. The last thing any of us wanted was the Park Police, Secret Service, and the Capitol District Police to discover people on the roof of the Lincoln Memorial at a time like this.

A few seconds later, there was a distant hair-raising scream! A heavy marble ceiling tile, the same one I had refused to cross just behind Lincoln's head, tipped and started to fall. I stared, with open-mouthed alarm as it hung there, and prayed no one was on top of it. We screamed to everyone and anyone, "Run! Get out of the way!"

A few seconds later the white tile fell, as if in slow motion. A corner of the marble rectangle glanced hard, off

Lincoln's right shoulder, bounced into the air, and descended to shatter on the pink marble floor, with a sound like a volley of gunshots. Thankfully, no one was in its path, except, poor, unsuspecting Lincoln himself.

Pandemonium followed. Visitors screamed, and bumped into each other trying to run away in confusion. Hordes of police ran up the steps with guns drawn yelling at them not to leave. Rangers ran over to the site of the crashed, and broken tile. In a panic, Christopher and his friends made their way back down to investigate the damage they had caused while Park Police stormed the stairwell, meeting them with guns drawn.

Christopher later reported that getting up on the roof went smoothly enough, but, climbing back down the ladder, the last person jumped from the second rung onto the board. It bowed, hitting the ceiling tile underneath, causing it to dislodge, and crash. At that point, Christopher knew he was, to say the very least, in serious trouble.

Bright and early the next day, Christopher had what very few rangers were able to arrange—a personal interview with James Ridenour, the Director of the National Park Service. His career as a ranger came to an abrupt end that morning, and poor Lincoln will forever have a chip on his shoulder.

·17·

The Wall of Names

One of the newest structures on the Mall, at the time, was the Vietnam Veteran's Memorial, more commonly known as The Wall. It had quickly become the most visited war memorial in the country. Due to the strong emotional charge, it was also the toughest location in which to work.

The physical make-up of the Wall with its long, stark, black granite face, carved with the names of over fifty-eight thousand Americans who died in Vietnam, brought visitors face-to-face in a new way, with the inescapable, hard reality, and sadness of war, and death. The wall made an open V shaped scar in the surrounding grassland which reminded me of the scars that war had inflicted on both our nation and Vietnam. Yet, its highly polished surface, reflected life—the sky, the surroundings, the visitors themselves.

The Wall inevitably evoked strong emotions in the thousands of people who stood before it each day, confronted with its unavoidable reality. Some felt anger, or fear, some intense sorrow. Tears of grief, of forgiveness, of guilt, of healing, were common. I often used to read the other rangers' log entries to try to fully comprehend, The Wall, but no entry was as powerful for me as my own personal, connection to The Wall.

I was 8 years old, in the third grade, and our class was abuzz about the upcoming Christmas holiday. The Principal came into our classroom during a math lesson, and asked our

teacher to follow him to the back of the room. I watched him whisper something in her ear. She froze as she broke into quiet tears. The room fell silent, and we all sat without moving as our teacher openly sobbed in the back of the room. What could have happened to make a grown-up cry?

After several minutes, she regained her composure, walked back to the front, and told us that our beloved Kindergarten teacher, Mrs. Petrashune, had a twenty-three-year-old son, Mike, who had been fighting over in Vietnam. She had just gotten word that he had been killed.

I was old enough to understand death, but not old enough then, to understand war, or the impact of the event, or even where, or what, Vietnam was. I did know that it was extremely sad, and that no one wanted to talk about it.

During my first assignment at The Wall, I looked up Mike's name, and found he was located on panel 06West, line 115 from the top. There it was: MICHAEL J. PETRASHUNE. Instinctively, I reached up to touch and trace his name with my fingers. To my surprise I found myself weeping. Although I didn't know Mike personally, I felt like a fraud as tears ran uncontrollably down my face, I did love his mom. It was for her, and for all the other grieving mothers that I wept. I leaned my forehead against the wall, and sighted along that endless line of names carved into black marble. Then I looked downward, and back to the left—more names without end. A new geography of grief gripped me. So many thousands of promising, young lives interrupted by this useless war—and for what?

I walked quickly back to the kiosk, and busied myself at something else, lest someone ask assistance from the ranger,

and find her a puddle of emotion. I spent the rest of my shift far away from The Wall. It took me several hours to come to grips with the immediacy of the emotions I felt for a person I didn't know, and for a war that I still did not understand.

One of our most solemn duties at The Wall was to pick up the artifacts left there, and catalog them. These ranged from letters, and Purple Heart medals, to teddy bears, and flowers. Once I heard that someone even left a Harley Davidson motorcycle with the license plate "HERO". For each, we recorded the date, time, names, Wall location, and item. Any perishable artifacts were recorded but thrown away. All others were carefully placed in a box to await transport to the Vietnam Veterans' Memorial warehouse. Sealed letters remained sealed, but open letters and notes were often read before going into the box. Much later many of the items would be part of an exhibit.

I especially remember one poignant, tear-stained, crumpled letter I read from a surviving soldier to his friend. "I wasn't able to go back for you," it said. "Enemy fire was all around me. I lost my sense of direction as I ran during the pull back. Pleading with our commander to go back was fruitless as it would have been a sure death sentence for all of us. So many times, I wish I were dead instead of living with the fact that I let you down. I let you die alone in that field. I have been living a muted life all these years. Please forgive me."

After that experience, I gave up studying about the site, and the details of the war, and started lending a compassionate ear to the visitors who could remain composed long enough to tell their stories. One rainy evening a middle-

aged woman approached the kiosk looking distressed. She had a piece of rubbing paper, and a pencil in her hands.

"Oh dear. I can't find my nephew William's name and our bus is loading, ready to leave. I *have* to find it."

We looked him up and as we walked quickly toward that section of the Wall, I was silent listening for the story behind the name.

"I'm here for my sister," she explained. "She's not in good health and couldn't travel from Illinois. It was her youngest son. I remember how he always wanted to be in the Army." She stopped for a moment, and the tears began. "He looked so proud, and handsome when he came home for a visit after basic training. It was just before he headed out to Vietnam."

I reassured her that the bus would not leave without her as we searched for his name. Then I noticed she was shivering, and had no raincoat. I took off my jacket, and placed it gently around her shoulders.

"It was so sad," she said and raised her chin, lips pressed together. "He was killed within the first month of being there. Most of his unit died that night."

Armed with the rubbing paper, we walked down The Wall, and I shared my own story. With a knowing look in her eye, she simply nodded. In the rain I watched her rub an impression of William's name for his mother in Illinois who would never forget him. I didn't know his aunt's name, nor she mine, but by sharing grief over the deaths of a useless war, both of us were healed a little that day.

·18·

The Haunting of the Jefferson Memorial

There are few places on the National Mall as magnificent as the Jefferson Memorial. I loved working there. Being in a space dedicated to one of the great minds of our country's founding, lends itself to contemplation, and reflection. I soon began to notice that the mood of the memorial transformed each night as the sun set. It was then, that the din of daytime visitors turned decorous. This memorial wasn't just another stop on the way to visit someplace else. One had to visit it by intention. It seemed people were genuinely interested in being there. The quality of visitors was different—more engaged—whether because of the man, the building, or the surroundings.

As an interpretive ranger, my talks would start with a resounding question that echoed around the central rotunda. "Who was Thomas Jefferson?" Answers ranged from President of the United States, to author of the Declaration of Independence, from architect, to slave owner. I told people that all those answers, and more, were accurate. Jefferson was a complex individual. He spoke five languages, and had great depth of knowledge in art, science, and math. He also had a deep understanding of nature.

It was he who had the foresight to purchase the Louisiana Territory and send Lewis and Clark on an expedition to figure out exactly what we had bought. I often imagined that the hushed, intense conversations in the Memorial would probably have had Jefferson smiling because

they indicated a level of thinking indicative of brilliant minds. At the very least, it was a reprieve from the all-too-shallow-but-important visitor question: "Where's the bathroom?"

I imagine that Jefferson, unlike Lincoln, would have liked his memorial. It was modeled after the Pantheon in Rome, and resembled Monticello, the beloved home he designed in Virginia. But there was always something strange about it. Many times, the sounds and wind that blew through the open chamber caught me off guard as if someone was whispering in my ear. When I stood at the foot of Jefferson's bronze statue, and gazed out toward the South Portico of the White House, I often saw large unexplained shadows dancing from the Memorial toward the White House lawn. It had been noted that Jefferson loved mocking birds. I would often hear them trilling on and on with their varied, and interesting songs. His memorial is the only place in D.C. that mocking birds have been sited on a regular basis. I soon came to suspect that Jefferson might be influencing shadows, and bird behavior from the great beyond.

There was always a time of day that I did not look forward to when working the evening shift—the midnight closing. Most people would be excited to end the late shift, and get home to sleep. But in order to do that, the Memorial's lower level had to be secured. It housed public bathrooms, and a private break room, and locker rooms for park personnel. These were kept locked, although there was nothing of particular value kept in the area. A strange nightly phenomenon would occur witnessed only by those ranger's brave, or unlucky enough to be called upon to lock up at the end of the midnight shift.

The Memorial was built in the 1930s when the United States desperately needed projects to get people back to work, and pull them out of the economic, and mental depression that had gripped the nation. It sits on reclaimed land from the depths of the Potomac River. The lower level rooms were always dank and musty due to an unfinished wall in the break room. This opening peered directly into the structural supports and dirt around the foundation. At first glance, I thought it was really exciting to think that I could explore the manmade cavern. What treasures might be discovered? Perhaps old tools discarded from a work crew eager to get on to the next Civilian Conservation Corps Project, or shells from the Potomac. Or even some graffiti. The possibilities were endless, but never explored, as I soon learned that to do so would have been at my own peril.

One night I walked over, and peered into the opening. The light cast by the half dozen 60-watt bulbs in the break room was absorbed in the darkness of the dirt floor. Shadows danced everywhere, and nowhere at the same time. A faint rhythmic howl of wind could be heard blowing through the cracks. The eerie underbelly of this building made sounds at night as if it were breathing. Goose bumps rose on the back of my neck. Intuitively, I felt a presence.

Could it have been the spirits of the workers who toiled to build a structure that represented the best of America, at a time when the country desperately needed uplifting? Or could it have been the spirit of Jefferson himself? Or perhaps Sally Hemings, his black mistress, had decided to claim her rightful spot in history by making her presence known? To this day I believe there was a life force that occupied the under

pinning of the Memorial, and that furthermore, it demanded respect.

My approach each night to the closing tasks of locking the doors, and turning off the lights downstairs became a game of wits—me against the unknown. I adopted a ten-step ritual, replete with respect for the non-physical, but leaving a bit of dignity for myself.

1. Tell a fellow ranger where you are going, and that if you aren't back in five minutes get down there, and come looking.
2. Take a deep breath as the iron door at the top of the stairs closes behind you.
3. Pick up speed with each successive step down the twenty-six stairs. At the bottom, peek around into the locker room, dart past the door, yell loudly, "Time to close up!"
4. Fling open the break room door, run through it, past the cavern opening to ensure the farthest door was locked.
5. Remember to breathe.
6. Run back through the break room, looking over your shoulder to make sure you are not being followed, or watched.
7. Turn off the lights.
8. Run upstairs as fast as your feet can take you.
9. Throw open the iron door, and jump through to safety.
10. Act like nothing has happened.

My method seemed to work as I lived to tell the tale.

(Author's Note: Upon my return to the Memorial in 2004, the lower level had been converted into a visitor center, complete with four walls, air conditioning, a bookstore, and new bathrooms. The eeriness was gone, but I couldn't help pondering what we lost in the process.)

Image courtesy of the U.S. Geological Survey (USGS)

·19·

A Monumental Thunderstorm

The National Mall is a Class A park. This means Rangers dress in Class A uniforms at all times. The Class A uniform consisted of wool pants, a polyester blend shirt, hat, and shined shoes. No shorts were allowed, even in the hot humid D.C. summers. None of the sites were air-conditioned. On 90-degree days we prayed to be assigned to the Washington Monument, since it was set up high on a hill than the rest of the Mall, and often had a nice steady breeze.

The downside of a summertime Monument assignment was we rotated once an hour into one of three unbelievably, hot areas: managing the line outside (no shade except for the styling hat), operating the elevator (25 people packed shoulder-to-shoulder for the slow 500-foot assent), and meeting the elevator up at the cramped, stuffy, and almost unbearably hot, glassed-in viewing level.

I loved how being a ranger let me explore little known parts of the building. After hours, I had access to the interior stairs that wind around to the top of the Monument. Since the 1970's, public access to the 898 steps had been closed due to the amount of vandalism to the commemorative stones, although guided tours took place during the summer.

The upper entrance to the stairway began at the 490-foot level. Often, I would choose to walk down after being on duty to escape the crowd. The massive walls absorbed any echo of my steps. The Monument is the largest freestanding

masonry structure in the world. This means it doesn't have support beams in the walls, which vary in thickness from six feet at the bottom, to 18 inches at the top.

The first hundred feet of the descent is well-lit with fluorescent lights. I always went slowly round and round, discovering the novelties that had been set in the stones of the interior walls, using my flashlight when the lighting became dim. There were 194 carved stones placed during the 40 years of construction from 1848 to 1888. The first stone set into the Monument in 1849 was from the state of Alabama. Alaska's stone, the last installed in 1982, was made of jade. There were stones representing every state in the union. Arizona's was made of petrified wood; Michigan's of native copper; Utah used its territorial name of Deseret. Also represented were cities, individual citizens, private companies, and surprisingly, foreign governments, such as Siam and Wales, as well as the Cherokee Nation.

In the beginning, there weren't any guidelines for the size of these decorative stones. As long as someone had the money and inclination, a stone was accepted for placement. Each marked stone had its own story to tell. It was like walking through history with every descended step. With every level I went down, the commemorative stones became more interesting in size, and character. My favorites were the fire departments stones, carved in the likeness of their coat of arms to display organizational strength and prestige.

I found out that in the early days, fire departments were civic organizations supported by donations from the community. In exchange for a donation, the donor would receive the coat of arms in metal, that was to be placed prominently over the front door to their home. There could be

several fire departments within a certain radius of any given home. If your building was on fire, and didn't have the proper coat of arms from the responding fire department, it would be left to burn until the 'right' fire department showed up, which gives a whole new meaning to 'buy local'!

Throughout the summer the rangers on duty at the top of the Washington Monument were always on the lookout for thunderstorms, and would use radio communication to the rangers at the bottom when they spotted storm clouds moving in. The Washington Monument happens to be the world's tallest lightening rod, and the last place that you'd ever want to be in a storm. The aluminum cap on the apex is surrounded by small steel rods, directly connected to the 520-foot elevator shaft, as a way of grounding the structure. Being in the elevator during a thunderstorm is the most dangerous place to be on the Mall, as you would, essentially, be inside of the lightening rod.

The mound the Monument sits on is the highest point with the largest open space, and therefore it is the second most dangerous place to be in a storm. The third most dangerous place, particularly for park personnel, was a small underground bunker, located at the western base of the Monument, and affectionately known as 'the pit'. This bunker was directly connected to the metal elevator shaft, and housed the controls for the massive lights that illuminated the Monument. During a storm, it was protocol to turn on the lights regardless of the time of day. This served many functions. If the storm was long lasting, it eliminated the need for personnel to make an additional, and potentially

dangerous, trip to the Monument to illuminate it, and the 50 flags that stand sentinel around the grounds.

Storms have a tendency to blow in quickly, leaving only enough time to race down the hill to the ranger station after evacuating everyone from the Monument. There were specific procedures for closing it down. The first priority was to get everyone out quickly and safely, which sometimes required two trips with the elevator. While the rangers at the top of the Monument hurry to herd people to elevator for the ride down, two other rangers secure the ground level, and make sure people outside the Monument are told to head to safety on lower ground. Another ranger descends to the 'pit' to turn on the lights.

One day in June, I was the Ranger assigned to 'pit' duty during an oncoming storm. The black clouds, thunder, and downpour were rolling in fast from the Southeast, so as soon as the decision was made to close the Monument, we all ran to take care of our assigned duties. I headed for the pit, pulled out my trusty F9 key (the universal key that opened every lock on the Mall), unlocked the master lock, and threw open the large iron mesh grate that covered the stairwell down to the bunker. I raced toward the circuit breaker panel that held four large switches. One by one I threw the red handles from the 'off' to the 'on' position. When my task was complete, I ran back up the stairs as fast as my feet would carry me, only to find the grate slammed shut again.

One of my comrades must have assumed I was on my way to the Ranger station, so they had closed and locked the gate to the pit stairs. The metal grate is constructed in such a way that the holes are too small for an adult's hand to reach through from underneath to get to the latch and unlock it. I

examined the mesh cage above my head that now held me captive with the hope of discovering a way to slip my hand through, and reach the lock. No go. There was no way I could free myself from the inside, even though I had a key. I didn't have a radio because I wasn't the Lead Ranger that day. With no way to communicate, and no way out, I was stuck at the bottom of the lightening rod. I listened for footsteps above, and tried yelling. Not a chance anyone would hear me, even if they were still there. Thunder rumbled, and the wind was beginning to roar.

"Don't panic," I told myself as I held onto the overhead gate of my prison, but my heart was racing. The crack of thunder was magnified down there. It seemed like a war zone. I went to stand in the middle of that concrete room, hoping it was safer. I closed my eyes and willed someone to notice that I was not among the rangers gathered safely downhill at Survey Lodge, the ranger station. Would I be safe if they didn't figure this out? It was one of my life's lonelier moments. I closed my eyes, and understood how helpless prisoners must feel when they are locked in their cells.

After what seemed an eternity, I thought I heard a faint voice over the scream of wind, and then hurried footsteps above. I yelled, and ran back to stare up through the grate. Yes, it was the face of a fellow ranger. He peered through with a look of panic, and called my name.

We both knew we had to act fast. With a quick turn of the key he unlocked the gate, and swung it open just enough for me to slip through. I ran up the stairs. We slammed the door, and jumped into the golf cart as the full downpour let loose. Clouds boiled overhead. He dodged forked lightening

and zoomed downhill to the ranger station while rain streamed over the brim of my hat and down my back.

Once safe inside, we turned to look at the Monument standing against the storm. In that moment a colossal blinding bolt of lightning struck the Monument, and exploded like multiple fireworks. We looked at one another, and blinked in disbelief. If we had been only half a minute later up there on the hill, we would have been toast!

·20·

The Georgia Stone

I answered a routine telephone call while awaiting site assignments for an evening shift.

"Hello. Survey Lodge."

"Hello. Is this the Park Service on the National Mall where the Washington Monument is located?" asked a soft male voice in the most endearing southern accent I had ever heard.

"Why yes, it is. How may I help you?"

"This is Eugene Massey from Georgia. I've been doing some genealogy research and I came across an emblem that I believe was the Georgia state symbol at one time. I understand that there are commemorative stones in the Washington Monument with the nineteenth century state symbols. Is that true?"

"Yes, sir. There are 194 stones dispersed throughout the interior of the Monument, and every state in the Union is represented. Most of them are from the latter half of the nineteenth century."

"Well, I was wondering if you would know what the stone from Georgia looks like? Is there an emblem on it?"

"Well now, it's been a while since I took a walking tour of the interior, but I must say it's one of my favorite things to do. Tell you what; I'm scheduled to be at the Monument in a couple of days. I'll bring my camera, and take some pictures of the Georgia stone so you can see for yourself

what it looks like. I don't remember what level it's located on, but I'll try to get the best lighting for the picture."

"Oh my, that would be so very kind of you. I'd greatly appreciate that favor."

I proceeded to get Mr. Massey's address so I could send him the photos.

Within a couple of days, while at the Washington Monument, I did walk down the interior stairs again, and found the Georgia stone at the 50-foot level. I wasn't hopeful of getting a good picture as the lighting is poor, and the walls are marred with years of patina, fingerprints, dirt and grime, not to mention the close quarters due to the thickness of the walls. When I took a deep breath, I could almost imagine a slight odor of horse manure, due to the fact that the incomplete Monument was used as a stable during the Civil War. Regardless, I held the camera in one hand, the flashlight in the other, and took several pictures hoping for the best. I had them developed, and they turned out rather well. I mailed them to Mr. Massey without thinking another thing about it. I was always happy to help with inquiries like that.

A couple of weeks later I was working at the Vietnam Veterans Memorial when the kiosk phone rang. It was highly unusual to get a phone call in the field, but I thought it might be one of the supervisors. Instead, it was a young man from Mrs. Fields Cookies looking for yours truly.

"Hello. I'm looking for a Helen Sis-ka-vich."

"Speaking."

"Um, okay, Miss. I have an order of cookies for you."

"You what?"

"Cookies. You know. What kind would you like?" He proceeded to list about ten kinds, one more delicious sounding than the next.

"Well, I'm sorry, I didn't order any cookies. I think you've got the wrong person."

"No Miss. I have the order right here. It's for a Helen from a Mr. Eugene Massey."

My mind raced back to the genteel man on the phone from Georgia. I was taken aback, as civil servants aren't supposed to accept gifts. Yet this was so completely charming. "Well then, how about—a white chocolate chip cookie," I said.

My response was greeted with silence on the other end.

"Ah, I think you don't understand. He's sent you four dozen cookies."

Now, it was my turn to be stunned. I knew these delicious cookies. One of Mrs. Fields cookies sold for about a dollar back then, and on a Park Ranger's salary, four dozen cookies were way over-the-top luxury.

"Uh, well, in that case, let's have…" and I proceeded to select a variety of favorites.

At our next meeting I shared my bounty with fellow rangers while I recounted the story of Mr. Eugene Massey and his search for the Georgia stone. I did send a follow up thank you note, all the while hearing that soft Georgia accent in my ear.

The Georgia Stone located at the 50' mark in the Washington Monument. "The Union as it was. The Constitution as it is."

·21·

Cherry Blossoms

Springtime is the most beautiful, and colorful time to visit Washington, D.C. thanks to the famous blossoming cherry trees around the Jefferson Memorial. Some of the rangers on the Mall wanted to start having nature walks. It seemed a bit odd to have a nature walk in the middle of the city, but the ulterior motive was to be able to leave the confines of the memorials for an hour or two, and enjoy a healthy walk.

Our focus was, naturally, the amazing cherry trees. In a collaborative effort, several interested Rangers researched facts about the trees, and practiced talks on each other in anticipation of leading groups around the Tidal Basin.

The cherry trees were a gift of friendship from Japan in 1910. However, the interest in bringing the trees to the United States started in 1885 when a woman named Eliza Scidmore, proposed having the trees planted on the newly reclaimed land along the Potomac. The U.S. Army Superintendent of the Office of Buildings and Grounds denied her proposal, as did every Superintendent for the next 24 years.

But Eliza Scidmore was persistent. She was a writer and photographer, a traveler to the countries of the Far East and the first female board member of the National Geographic Society. She started fundraising, and ran a letter writing campaign, which included a letter to First Lady, Mrs. Helen Taft. Getting the attention of the First Lady proved fruitful.

In January 1910, two thousand cherry trees from Japan finally arrived in America, but Eliza's triumph was short lived. Inspectors declared that the trees were infected. Politically, it was a tricky situation. President Taft had the delicate job of informing the Emperor of Japan that his generous gift of trees were diseased and had to be destroyed to protect American growers.

In a magnanimous gesture, the mayor of Tokyo agreed to raise over 3,000 trees, cultivated specifically to be hardy, as well as disease, and insect free. In March 1912, the new trees arrived in Washington. As she watched the planting, Eliza Scidmore could hardly have imagined what beauty her inspired vision would bring to our country seventy years later.

I wandered among the pink blossoming trees, and found their sheer number, and surpassing beauty evoked the same deep emotion and awe I'd had in the western desert. I was inspired, moved, and touched thinking about the vision and persistence that had left such a legacy for us all. How many millions of people have enjoyed the gentle beauty of the flowering trees without giving a thought to the person behind the movement to get them planted? How selfless was her gift? She carried on for so many years with little encouragement. And what would Eliza think of the admiring crowds now?

The sheer volume of cherry trees all in full bloom around the Reflecting Pool had a deep effect on visitors—so much so that some wanted to carry a little piece of D.C. home with them, or at least until the blossoms wilted, and they tired of lugging around a tree branch. As Park Rangers, we took an oath to 'preserve and protect' the resources for future generations. Part of our interpretive talks always included

information on the possible consequences of removing anything from the site. The fines could include a monetary judgment and/or imprisonment.

On one particularly beautiful, and balmy spring day, the sidewalk around the Tidal Basin was crowded with people. Their visit had coincided with the annual Cherry Blossom Festival. It was time to don my hat and drum up business for the nature walk I had been preparing. I felt like a pied piper as I led a tour of 20 people through the trees. Cherry blossoms fell gently around us like soft, pink, snow, and the waters rippled under a blue, spring sky. I gave the standard spiel about protecting resources for future generations, and made sure the people on the tour understood, that by picking the cherry blossoms, or breaking branches off the trees, they were destroying a precious resource—an action punishable by fines, or even imprisonment.

The tour was going well. People were engaged in the conversation about Eliza Scidmore, Japan, and the history, as well as some natural tidbits about cherry trees. They were generally appreciating the beauty that surrounded them. At certain spots along the route we stopped, as I pointed out several items of interest, allowing the slower walkers to catch up. Sometimes our attendance would swell, as other visitors joined us.

Several people not connected to our group were a few feet ahead of us. One of the women reached up, grabbed a branch, proceeded to twist, and break it off. Since her back was to me, she didn't see me as I calmly walked up, and said loud enough for all to hear, "Ma'am, you are destroying a

national natural resource by breaking that branch off the tree. How many days would you like to spend in jail?"

The woman's eyes darted around, and I could see she was horrified at being caught, stared down by 20 outraged people, and a Park Ranger. She turned away clutching the branch to her breast, and walked briskly in the other direction. Then she stopped and spun around. With the entire muster of a two-year-old, she stuck out her tongue as if to say, "I don't care. I'll do whatever I want, and you can't stop me!" Then, she turned, and ran away. When working with the public, you never know what you're going to encounter. A ranger has to be prepared for grown-ups who act like misbehaving toddlers.

The entire tour group was aghast.

I chuckled. "Well, I guess she told me, didn't she?"

There were smiles as we walked on.

·22·

Project R.U.M.

What do McDonald's, Dow Chemical, and the National Parks have in common? Upon further thought, *how* did McDonald's, Dow Chemical, and the National Parks come to have anything in common? The mission, at least for the first two, seemed an unlikely fit for cleaning up the environment, but the phrase "reduce, reuse, recycle" had become popular in the early 90s. It seemed people were finally aware of the amount of waste being generated. A new term for companies was emerging: *the double bottom line.*

The plastic industry, in particular, was getting an increased amount of scrutiny. Plastic was suffering from an image problem. Were things being over packaged? What if the package ended up in the garbage destined for a long life in an overflowing landfill?

By 1990, a decade old practice, McDonald's had packaged its sandwiches in beautifully decorated Styrofoam clamshells. It was a technological breakthrough in fast food. This little container held heat longer, and extended the sandwich's shelf life while awaiting consumption. Dow Chemical made the plastic that went into the Styrofoam, but consumer pressure was beginning to build around McDonald's packaging.

What could be done to turn the image problem around?

Someone at Dow had a brilliant idea. "What about a public/private partnership?" Once that core thought was

developed, it was only a matter of Who, What, Where, When and How.

Who turned out to be the National Parks. *What* was a recycling program. *Where* would be The Great Smokey Mountains, The Grand Canyon, Yosemite, Acadia, The Everglades, Mt. Rainer—and the National Mall. *When* was over a two-year period. *How* would be accomplished with seven million dollars in seed money.

Would that be enough to turn around the image problem of plastics by recycling them? Time would tell.

If anyone should lead the environmental charge, it was the Park Service. The heart of their mission is to preserve and protect resources. Tens of millions of people visited our National Parks at the time, and the amount of trash generated was similar to a city. Some of our parks were literally being buried in trash.

Dow's seed money was what the parks needed to get their recycling programs off the ground.

The National Mall, the most highly visited of the urban parks, was the last to receive the money, and support.

I had already been gung-ho about recycling. It had become my personal intention to start a recycling program on the Mall. I stayed up late, and read everything I could about the subject. I talked with other like-minded people in the EPA and Forest Service, and over the months, grew to be known as an expert on the topic of recycling.

I named what we were doing Project R.U.M. – Recycling Upon the Mall.

It just so happened; my interest coincided with the timing of the Dow seed money. I was asked to be the

'champion' for the program within the park. This meant that I would help train other rangers, meet with the Dow partners to discuss ideas on how best to implement the program, and help develop the messaging that would impact success.

My experience as a field ranger on the Mall, had given me the opportunity to observe many things over a period of time—things like human behavior, traffic patterns, and daily visitation order. I also had a lot of time to take informal surveys on people's attitudes about recycling. What I discovered was that people really wanted to do the right thing. They also didn't want to be too inconvenienced while doing the right thing.

There were multiple challenges to implementing a recycling program on the Mall. Most concession stands used plastic coated paper cups. There was the dilemma of how to keep the waste stream clean. How do you have separate containers, and have only recyclables in one, and only trash in the other? Retraining the public would take time. Messaging was important, with signage being critical, especially when there are politically sensitive sites on the Mall like the Vietnam Veterans Memorial. How could we acknowledge the contribution of Dow Chemical around this Memorial without raising eyebrows, or opening old wounds?

I had to meet each challenge head on. Someone decided that the plastic-coated paper cups should be replaced with polystyrene. Gasp! The very thing that went into McDonald's clamshells were now being integrated on the National Mall! How could that be? One simple word—*market.* There simply wasn't a market to recycle plastic coated paper cups. There wasn't even a process to reverse engineer these cups. They were simply trash once the contents

were consumed. There *was*, however, a market for polystyrene—at least a small, budding market.

Keeping the waste stream clean was challenging. Although there was trash, and recycling bins near one another, with crystal clear signage, there was still contamination. Over time, the public caught on. Luckily, the Park Service wasn't the only agency working on retraining the public. There was a government-wide effort to educate.

We handled the politically sensitive Vietnam Veterans Memorial site by simply having recycling bins with signage with the familiar recycling symbol. All of the other bins throughout the park had the symbol, as well as 'in partnership with Dow Chemical'. At least, it was low key.

I felt fortunate to be involved with this program. It was exciting, fast moving, and world changing, even on a personal level. I was asked to be on a temporary work detail at the National Park Service's Washington Office, or WASO as we affectionately called it. It was at this level where national policies were created. Notice – I didn't say implemented. It is always easier to create a policy than to implement it. One of my first assignments was to put together an informational display for a government agency national conference about what the parks were doing with their recycling program. It felt wonderful to be taking action on my passion, and to collaborate with people within other government agencies, such as the Forest Service, the EPA and the Post Office. I was riding a high wave of momentum, and loving every minute of it. What had started out as a six-week project turned into a year-long job where I helped get the Park's national recycling program off the ground. Was

recycling implemented in all 357 park sites by the time I left the assignment? No. But we had a good start.

Creating change within a government agency takes persistence, and commitment. As a seasoned National Park Ranger told me, "The wheels of government turn, but they turn slowly. Be patient, consistent, and persistent."

Even after my success, due to a change in the political climate, I returned to being an ordinary ranger on the Mall.

Looking back, it's been over twenty years since my involvement with Project R.U.M. and the National Parks as a Ranger. I am extremely satisfied to know that the best thing about the project is that the world has come to claim recycling as its own.

Getting recycling bins ready for the
4th of July crowds, 1994.
Location: Washington Monument

·23·

Definite Maybe, Ask Me in a Month

I drove into Survey Lodge parking lot one day to start my shift, and noticed a light blue, extended cab, long bed Chevy pickup with New Mexico plates. This huge truck seemed to take up two coveted parking spaces, but in reality, it simply filled one *entire* parking space. Most of my ranger colleagues drove subcompacts or used public transportation, so the truck looked particularly out of place.

I parked my car in the one remaining space beyond this behemoth, climbed out, and inspected it. The interior was tidy and clean, and the bed of the truck was filled with house plants. How odd those plants looked in a truck like that, I thought. Or maybe interesting. Roll call was about to start, so I hustled into the building expecting I might see the owner of the truck, but it turned out the new ranger was in with the supervisor getting orientated.

For two weeks, I was left to wonder about this stranger in a strange land.

"So, Bill," I asked a compatriot one evening. "What can you tell me about the guy who drives the monster truck from New Mexico?"

"He's a seasonal ranger, a rookie, why?"

"I figured that much out for myself, thanks!" I laughed.

"His name's John, I think. Don't remember his last name. Looks to be about 30. Not sure about anything else. He was concerned about those houseplants, though they all

seemed to survive the trip from New Mexico." He looked over his shoulder with a coy smile. "You seem interested. Shall I tell him?"

"Can't a girl be interested in new recruits?" I tried to look neutral. Was I interested?

Two days later, the new ranger and I had an opportunity to work together at the Washington Monument. I played it cool, and pretended I didn't know a thing about him. Why was my heart racing as I approached him? This was uncomfortable, not at all like me. I was usually so well defended.

"Hi. My name is Helen. You must be the new ranger."

"Yes," he said and stuck out his hand. "John Hossley. Nice to meet you, Helen."

"I noticed your truck. It's a monster for the city. Do you have trouble finding parking?"

"Not really. I just drive around and around the block until I finally find a space I can pull into. It breeds patience," he said. His smile certainly was handsome, I was thinking—and maybe trying not to think.

"Have you been in the city long?"

"No, I just arrived a few days ago. I'm staying with friends until I can find a place."

"Have you been here before?"

"Oh, just once as a young child, and I don't remember anything about the visit. And once for training, when I worked for Marriott, but I never got to see the city. I was so disappointed, I decided to come back someday. So here I am."

We talked for a few more minutes until we had a rotation shift. I kept breaking into smiles for the rest of the evening. He was easy to talk to and we shared a keen interest in history, and in exploring the city.

Our paths didn't cross again for a week. I was sitting in Survey Lodge waiting for roll call when John walked in.

"Hi" he said turning to me. A smile spread across his face. "Can I buy you a Coke?"

"No thanks, I already have a Pepsi."

He sat next to me. "Well, in that case, what if I asked you to lunch?"

"I'd probably say yes."

We met at Union Station for lunch, then visited the National Museum of Modern Art. John told me that first lunch felt like the Grand Inquisition. I asked question after question because I was so nervous.

"How many brothers and sisters?" "Nine. I'm the youngest of ten."

"What are your parents like?" "Tired. After ten kids."

"Any hobbies?" "I like plants and history."

"Where have you travelled?" "Mostly out west. I considered joining the Merchant Marine, but realized I don't like boats, so I applied to the Park Service instead."

"What part of New Mexico are you from?" "A little town in the south, called Deming."

"Did you go to college?" "New Mexico State University in Las Cruces."

"What parts of history interest you most?" "World War II, and Winston Churchill. My parents met during the war. My father was a doctor and my mother was a nurse in his unit."

I kept tossing questions his way to keep him from asking me any.

I couldn't have been too intimidating as we did exchange phone numbers.

On our first real date we drove up to Gettysburg to study the battlefields. Neither of us had been there before, and we thought it would be a good opportunity to find common interests, and do research for our talks at the Lincoln Memorial. John offered to drive. His truck had a bench seat, and he patted the space next to him. I surprised myself by sliding over, and not resisting when he held my hand. What was this? Why did this man feel so safe?

We stopped at the visitor center to get oriented, stared at the large battlefield map, and agreed on a point of interest. Arriving at our destination, John jumped out of the truck first. I was trying to roll up the window by turning the crank handle on the driver's side when he pulled open the door, and lifted me out.

"I hate suspense," he said, and kissed me before I could pull away. It was more like a quick peck on the lips, but that was enough. I felt a giant spark ignite between us.

Our afternoon together was fun, effortless, breathtaking, and joyful. I was floating on air the rest of the trip. I knew I had met THE ONE. Just like that. I had hit the jackpot on my first real date, even if it took me 30 years. For once I didn't analyze my feelings or question them. I let my heart do the thinking.

"Well, now what?" he asked as we drove back to D.C.

"What do you mean?"

"Clearly, we like each other and I want to see more of you, but we do work together." he said.

"Why would that be a problem? We're equals. Neither of us is subordinate to the other."

"Well, I think we shouldn't be at the same site."

"Let's just see how the rotations go. If we find we're placed together too much, we can just ask for a different site during roll call."

We spent the rest of the drive back to D.C. in easy conversation. Neither of us wanted the day to end so we found a Mexican restaurant to prolong the day. It was around eleven when we realized we were the only people in the restaurant besides the impatient staff. We paid our bill, drank the rest of our margaritas, and worked our way to the parking lot. This time our kiss was prolonged, and sensual, but only a prelude to an amazing goodnight kiss at the door of my apartment.

"Wow! Could this day have been any better?" I said, and finally pulled away from his émbrace.

"Not by my standards that's for sure."

"Drive home safely."

The instant the truck rounded the corner, I raced back into my apartment, and looked at the clock. Good, only 11:30, so it was 8:30 on the west coast. There was only one person I wanted to talk to. I picked up the phone, my fingers were shaking as I dialed.

"Oh Ginger!" I exclaimed before she even said hello.

"Helcat? It's been way too long. What's up these days?"

I knew she could feel my ear-to-ear smile, and hear the excitement in my voice.

"I've met the most wonderful man. I think he's THE ONE!"

"Oh, really? This is just a bit of a turnaround. Tell me every juicy detail."

I proceeded to tell her about John, his family, his plants, and our first real date.

"So, you've basically decided he's THE ONE after the first date?" she asked with skepticism in her voice.

"I can't explain it rationally, but yes! Do you get it? He's the reason I needed to be back in D.C. It's so utterly amazing. When John and I were comparing life stories, we lived and worked in the same states at the same time. Our lives have been following each other. He worked for Marriott out of college. *I* worked for Marriott after college. He lived in Florida and worked on an internship in the summer of '81. *I* lived in Florida, work on an internship in the summer of '81. He lived in Colorado in the 80's and worked at Vail. *I* travelled to Colorado several times in the 80's and skied at Vail. He's from New Mexico and well, you know how I've always wanted to spend more time there!" I laughed as I heard myself babbling.

"I'm incredibly happy for you Helcat."

"Me too." I said with tears in my eyes. "It took me way long, but I made it."

I hung up the phone, and thought about the important conversation Ginger and I shared a year and a half before at the hostel in Silverton, Colorado. I barely recognized myself.

Since then, I had developed a confidence, as if I had grown into the woman I'd always wanted to be. Here I was, allowing myself to take a chance on love—both loving myself as well as another person. At that moment, I granted myself the freedom to explore the emotional highs and lows that would come. There was no need to hide any more, to guard or run away from my fear. I had an inexplicable sense that all would be well.

Falling in love on the National Mall in the summertime is magical, especially at night. The meticulously placed lighting around buildings and walkways enhances the beauty, and lends a quiet romantic luminosity.

John and I spent as much time together as we could. Initially, we did find ourselves working at the same sites, usually the Washington Monument. From time-to-time I convinced him to steal away, and walk down the steps of the Monument so that we could be alone. Occasionally, I would jump into the elevator while John was the operator, and kiss him before visitors were allowed on. It was fun, but we both knew that we should be separated while at work in order to do our jobs well. So, we informed our supervisors that we were in a relationship, and requested not to work at the same site. We arranged to have our dinner breaks together.

One warm summer evening I was making my way from the Washington Monument toward the Lincoln Memorial along the gravel pathway near the reflecting pool. I was planning to meet John for dinner on our favorite bench. A young boy about seven years old approached me, walking by himself with his hands behind his back. I was concerned, as I

didn't see a parent close by. I walked up to the boy, knelt down, and asked if he was lost.

At first, he seemed confused, then embarrassed, then he smiled, and pulled a beautiful red rose from behind his back, and handed it to me.

Stunned, I took the rose. "Why, thank you." I said still trying to figure out the mystery when I looked up, and noticed his mother peering out from behind one of the trees with a bright smile. She caught up to her son, and lifted him into her arms.

"It's not every day that you can help spark young love," she said, "especially young love in ranger uniforms."

At that moment, I looked up and saw John walking toward me with a huge smile. Mother and son watched me run to give him a big hug and kiss, and then turned and walked away. John and I sat on a nearby bench to share our usual dinner date, complete with peanut butter and jelly sandwiches.

At the end of June, Ginger was back on the east coast visiting her mother, and making plans for her September wedding to Keith when I stopped in to see her on my way back to D.C. from visiting my parents.

"I think John is going to ask me to marry him when I get back." I said in a matter of fact tone.

"Oh really?" she said. "That's big. But you make it sound kind of un-big."

"No, it's just that I'm having such a good time, I'm not sure that I want to be married."

"Well, you'll figure all that out." She had more faith in me than I did.

We chatted like two old friends do, and she filled me in on her pending nuptials.

I arrived back in D.C. in time for the 4th of July. It was 'all rangers on deck' during this huge event. We were required to work an 18-hour day as hundreds of thousands of people converged on the National Mall to witness and experience the best fireworks display in the country. John and I had a glamorous assignment for the day: babysitting a VIP parking lot. It was a temporary lot on the southwest side of the Lincoln Memorial for those who had pull in the Department of the Interior, and didn't want to fight for a parking space. To keep boredom at bay, we played games, read, and did parameter patrols as we walked along the reflecting pool toward the Lincoln Memorial.

During our dinner break, John seemed nervous. We sought refuge from the crowds by sitting on the grass near the little visited World War I Memorial.

He took a small box out of his pocket.

I glanced down at it, suddenly nervous, then back up at him.

"Helen, I can't believe how lucky I am to have you in my life. You're a dream come true. I dreamed of you so many years, and now God has sent an answer to my prayers. I never realized how lonely I was before I met you. You're smart, and fun to be around. You have a wonderful sense of humor, and I believe you're the most beautiful girl to come out of the state of New York. I would love to be your husband. Will you marry me?"

It took my breath away, the distance between the raw uncertain place I had been in a year ago, and now this. I

needed time to process it all. Could I tell him this was my first relationship with a man? So, I said, "Definite maybe. Ask me in a month."

In an instant I saw that I had crushed his heart.

"What does that mean?" he asked.

"Well, I think I really enjoy my life as a single person, and I'm not sure that I want to be married. But if I wanted to be married, you'd be the man. I guess I need to figure out if I want to be married."

For two days, I mulled the big question from every angle. Do I remain single and continue to date John, even though knowing him had changed me forever? Getting married so soon didn't make any sense intellectually. We both admitted that neither of us had had a long-term relationship before. I was John's first girlfriend ever, and he was my first boyfriend. He explained that having a girlfriend as a teen or young adult had just seemed too stressful. He didn't want to deal with the angst, and he had too many other things to do. But it hadn't taken him even a week to decide with absolute certainty that I was the one for him.

We were clueless in this new land we were traveling together, and sometimes it's better that way. Some things are beyond what the mind can understand.

On July 6, while feasting alone on a bean burrito at Taco Bell, and mulling the growing to-marry-or-not-to-marry dilemma, a thought lit up my mind. "I know what it's like to be single, and it's great. Who says married life can't be just as great?" And right then, I decided that I would marry John. All I had to do was tell him.

I arrived early at Survey Lodge the next day, and put up a sign in the entry hall that read in big letters: "YES, JOHN, I WILL MARRY YOU!"

When the other rangers noticed me taping up my answer, the room was abuzz with excitement, and questions. "When did he ask?" "Where did he propose?" "Who won the bet?"

When all of their questions were answered, they calmed down.

John walked in the door ten minutes later. I was sitting under my sign, with a bright smile. He did not notice me or anyone else in the room. He slumped past looking still forlorn about my previous answer to his personal policy change proposal. Then someone yelled, "Hey John, back up! Look. Over there."

The moment of surprise was captured perfectly on film. With hugs, tears, and a swell of "Congratulations!" the two of us journeyed out of Survey Lodge to enjoy the thrill of our happiest moment.

With the acceptance of the life-changing proposal, I entered the unfamiliar world of compromise. I wanted a fall wedding because what is more beautiful than foliage season in the Adirondacks? But I didn't think four months would be enough time to plan. Besides, my family didn't even know I was dating yet. So, we made arrangements for time off, and took a trip back to Lyon Mountain.

"John and I will set a date soon," I promised as we pulled out of the driveway to make our way back to D.C.

For the next several weeks, John and I batted dates back and forth with no resolution. The indecision was getting a little tense.

"Okay, tonight let's each look at a calendar, pick a date, and we'll discuss it over dinner tomorrow. Deal?" I asked.

"Deal," he said.

That night we both presented our dates. And remarkably we both had the same date— February 29, 1992!

"Hey, it's such a perfect date," I said getting excited. "When people ask how long we've been married, we'll tell them we're still newlyweds since our actual anniversary will be once every four years!"

"Yes, and we can celebrate the entire month of February, and the first day of March every year instead of one day," John added. He was beaming.

When I told my mother the date, there was dead silence on the other end of the phone.

"What?" I asked.

"That's the dead of winter up here. What if it snows three feet?"

"If we're lucky, it will." I said.

On February 28th a snowstorm did drop three feet of snow in the Adirondacks! John and I got married the next day regardless of 20 below zero weather, and snow banks piled seven feet high. Our wedding pictures captured the winter wonderland, and our reception at the Hotel Saranac was so much fun that it was still talked about two decades later.

After our honeymoon to Quebec City and New Mexico, we embraced our new life together in D.C. We continued to work as Park Rangers. I had several months left on my special recycling program assignment at the Washington Office of the Park Service and John stayed on The Mall.

Our wedding day, February 29, 1992

"Rangers in Love" ©1991 John & Helen

·24·

Once a Ranger, Always a Ranger

I loved being a National Park Ranger. I loved the mission. I enjoyed the creativity, adventure, and learning that were part of being an interpretative ranger. I found meeting interesting people from all over the world very stimulating. In my special assignment I had the opportunity to travel to various parks within the system, and was beginning to establish professional relationships.

It would have been my dream come true if the special recycling assignment had been made into a permanent position. Alas, such positions within the Park Service were extremely hard to come by under normal circumstances, and in 1992 things were changing in a big way. There was great hope and anticipation for environmental causes with Bill Clinton's incoming administration. I discovered that many activities within the government grind to a halt when there is a change in the White House. The creation of new positions was stopped until the new administration could study the issues. My special assignment ended, and I went back to the National Mall.

For a time, John and I contemplated making a career out of the Park Service. He offered to apply for permanent positions at other sites, and said he would follow me wherever I wanted to go, although he didn't like government bureaucracy any more than I did. We began to realize that the reality of finding two positions in the same place, with the possibility of permanent status within the Park System was

remote. If we were lucky enough to land temporary positions in another park, working our way into permanent status would take about five years, a time frame that seemed like an eternity at the time.

John decided to leave the Park Service after a year of employment. I continued for a couple more years. I was holding out hope that I would be called back to the recycling coordinator position. When I realized that was not going to happen, I did a hard assessment of my talents and desires.

Was being a National Park Ranger the best job I'd ever had? Absolutely. My years as a Ranger had shaped me in ways I never imagined. For instance, I discovered my love of public speaking, and telling stories; I came to realize that I had a knack for producing unprecedented results in projects that I took on. Big ideas energized me then, and they still do.

The question became, would I be willing to work over a period of years toward the coveted permanent status? Not really. I believed that I could accomplish more, and have more flexibility with my project management abilities outside of the government.

Since my employment with the National Park Service, I have used my project management abilities as CEO of the Vermont Association of Realtors®; help reduce energy use by millions of kilowatt hours on dairy farms across America; gotten bonds passed to fund energy efficient upgrades to our local schools, and organized fundraising and construction of playgrounds across my new hometown of Burlington, Vermont.

After twenty-five years, I still consider myself a ranger because I have not forgotten the rich experience of wearing the hat. I have realized that being a ranger is a state

of mind and attitude that has carried me throughout my life, whether it be walking in a park with my children; telling them creative stories to explain things, or appreciating the beauty of nature. I often ask myself, "What if everyone treated the world as if it was a National Park?"

In my own way, I've continued with the Park Service mission of preserving and protecting for future generations. Lofty ideals, and completely worth striving for. It's a code that continues to inform my actions.

At Glen Canyon National Recreation Area circa 1990

Epilogue

Ginger Farrar Rivenbark and I have remained lifelong friends. Our lives have had a similar trajectory. She married Keith in September 1991. We have children the same ages and are empty nesters. She lives in Albuquerque, New Mexico.

Ginger and I had a reunion hike of the Havasupai Reservation area of the Grand Canyon in 2007. We agree that we live too far away from each other, and wish we were neighbors. We are planning our next adventures. On the list are: an Alaskan cruise, a week-long cross-country ski adventure in Yellowstone, and sipping margaritas on a tropical island beach.

In 1994, John and I moved to Burlington, Vermont to fulfill John's dream of living in New England. I reconnected with my family, and the North Country of New York. We will celebrate our 7th Anniversary (28 years) in February 2020. We raised two incredibly, wonderful, young women who continue to amaze us with their intellect, humor, and desire to follow their passion. We are proud parents.

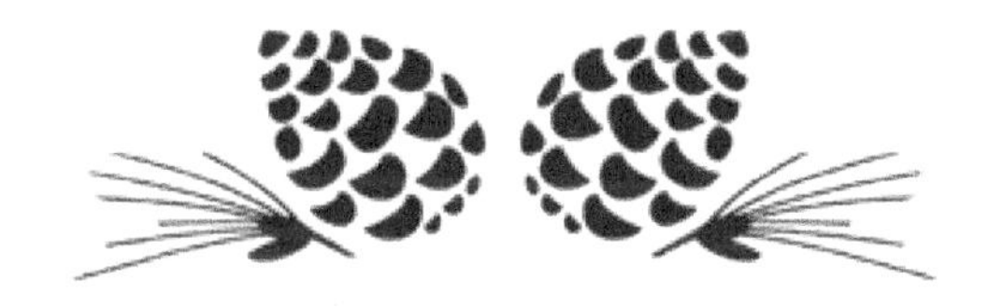

Made in United States
North Haven, CT
18 June 2023